Frank S

C000149902

Copyright © 1998 Omnibus Press
(A Division of Book Sales Limited)

Edited by Chris Charlesworth
Cover & Book designed by Hilite Design & Reprographics Limited
Picture research by Nikki Russell

ISBN: 0.7119.6624.9
Order No: OP48014

Exclusive Distributors:
Book Sales Limited, 8/9 Frith Street, London W1V 5TZ, UK.
Music Sales Corporation, 257 Park Avenue South, New York, NY 10010, USA.
Music Sales Pty Limited, 120 Rothschild Avenue, Rosebery, NSW 2018, Australia.

To the Music Trade only:
Music Sales Limited, 8/9, Frith Street, London W1V 5TZ, UK.

Photo credits: Front cover and all other pictures supplied by LFI.

Every effort has been made to trace the copyright holders of the photographs in this book but one or two were unreachable. We would be grateful if the photographers concerned would contact us.

Printed in the United Kingdom by: Ebenezer Baylis & Son, Worcester.

A catalogue record for this book is available from the British Library.

Visit Omnibus Press at http://www.musicsales.co.uk

OMNIBUS PRESS
LONDON · NEW YORK · SYDNEY

Contents

Introduction

The invention of the gramophone record revolutionised the way popular music could be experienced. No longer was it of necessity handed down from one folk artist to another, or coldly reconstructed from sheet music or piano rolls. As the record and radio industries developed in parallel during the Twenties, music could be instantly disseminated across continents, and 'stars' were created remote from their live performances. The first artists to benefit from this were the female 'classic blues' singers of that decade, of whom the greatest was Bessie Smith. Thirty years later Elvis Presley became the best-selling artist in the United Kingdom, but his physical presence in the country was limited to one brief stopover while changing planes in Scotland. His voice on record, his image in the cinema and his photo in the fanzines were enough.

In terms of fan reaction and career longevity, Frank Sinatra is undoubtedly the biggest star of the recording era, and therefore of the 20th century. He was there long before Presley, and long after him. Most admirers would also accord Sinatra the ultimate creative as well as commercial accolade, and nominate him as the greatest ever interpreter of popular song. Bing Crosby was already a star when Sinatra began his career, but to Crosby's mellow crooning Sinatra added sex appeal and a hard-edged jazz discipline. Of course Crosby survived triumphantly, just as Bill Haley wasn't immediately put out of work by the dangerous Presley, but once the mature Sinatra style developed in the Fifties Crosby seemed cosier, less 'hip', a comforting representative of the old order. His great talent was to relax, to soothe, to exploit the art of crooning as some sort of healing process. While Crosby relaxed the senses, Sinatra alerted and challenged them.

It may be that Sinatra was the first pop singer to see himself consciously as a creative artist - he had something to say, and the lyrics and the melodies of the writers, the arrangements of Axel Stordahl, Nelson Riddle or Gordon Jenkins, these were his canvas and paint, his camera, his typewriter. Before him, if we pursue this line, vocalists were at heart vaudeville entertainers, however blessed with genius. But Sinatra created, built something new.

A lesser performer would sing a happy song, for example, without evoking anything beyond its optimistic jauntiness. It would exist in a show-business vacuum, filed under 'good time'. Sinatra went further. In real life, after all, happiness is always tempered by the knowledge that it must end - Sinatra could always find a hidden reef of melancholy in the bright pool of sun-dappled water.

This might come over as part of a 'set 'em up, Joe' persona, the saloon singer who he occasionally described himself as with rare self-effacement. It could be reflected in a big-lunged legato exploration of a previously-straightforward melody line. It could be in the careful building up of an album that is so much

more than the sum of its parts - or in all of these. However he does it, the non-composer Sinatra is writing his songs, colouring his backdrops, capturing scenes, using someone else's raw materials. His legato technique, holding a note, bending it, shading it into the next, eliding a sequence together without apparently pausing for breath, was in itself a departure. Previous popular singers, led, of course, by Crosby, had used syncopation, the jaunty rhythmic drive against the beat that drives a song along.

No-one before Sinatra had interpreted the material in his way, but everyone who has worked in the mainstream of popular music since his great days on the Capitol label in the Fifties has had to be aware of Sinatra's technique. When he started in the business the brief career of the Mississippi blues singer Robert Johnson was coming to a violent conclusion. After Johnson, the country blues had new depths of feeling, passion and guilt available to it, while Billie Holiday brought similar range to its urban cousin. At the other extreme, far from the dirt fields of Mississippi, Crosby had moved a jazzman's grasp of a tune into the mainstream, a syncopated style of 'riding' a melody.

The mature Sinatra was neither a blues wailer nor a crooner, though he hinted at elements of both. But the blues in his music comes through in his command of mood, not in his technical skill at the blues form where - in his understandably rare attempts - he can sound somewhat unbending, even uncertain. Nevertheless he has named Billie Holiday as his greatest single influence, and Crosby - later to be a friend - was at very least an influence in a negative manner, in that the ambitious young Sinatra realised intuitively that he would have to approach songs in a different way from Crosby. It might be observed at this point that Sinatra's tentativeness with the blues was also apparent in his occasional stabs at that other root of black music, gospel.

His uniqueness was in his ability to climb inside a lyric and a melody, to worry at the words and explore the notes, sometimes employing the technique of inserting an unscored extra note to weld two melodic notes together, and to express whatever emotion or technical ingenuity that he came across in a semi-detached, almost quizzical manner. He neither screamed out in an ecstasy of passion like Johnson, nor bounced the song playfully around like Crosby. He reinvented the material, turning alike a work of art by Gershwin and a production-line Tin Pan Alley tune into a new Sinatra discovery.

Contrast this with the style of one of his rivals at the outset of his career, Bob Eberle. The latter sounds only quaint today, the product of a distant age, the music of which no longer has any relevance. Eberle sang of love as a storybook ideal, whereas Sinatra sang of it as a real-life experience. His art was conveyed in nuance, inflection.

The music critic Will Friedwald has noted that George Gershwin (1937), Lorenz Hart (1943) and Jerome Kern (1945) died in the years that saw Sinatra establishing his reputation. Did this prompt a conscious decision on the part of the young singer to preserve their work? In his youthful arrogance he would certainly have aimed at 'definitive' versions.

And it can certainly be said with only slight exaggeration that Sinatra pioneered the concept of the 'standard' in popular music. Of course others, notably Crosby, had occasionally revived a time-tested song, but the pre-Sinatra music industry was almost entirely fuelled by the constantly-turning machinery of Tin Pan Alley, feeding the vocalists' desire to be the first with the latest tunes. Throughout Sinatra's career, by contrast, a hefty proportion of his concert repertoire was drawn from the great decade of the American popular song, from the mid-Thirties onwards.

Sinatra once referred to the Italian operatic style of bel canto ('beautiful singing') in connection with his voice, but without claiming any shared technique. Given his justifiably self-confident assessment of his prowess as a song stylist, he was probably evoking a classical discipline without wishing the comparison to be examined too closely.

Certainly it is hard to hear any trace of operatic singing in his voice - he cannot sing an aria, because its formality stifles all his vocal trump cards. And, in spite of his proud adherence to his immigrant father's name, Sinatra was a full-blooded American. He never learned to speak Italian, and showed little interest in the classical music of his ancestral country. In fact, his voice has few traces of any vocal style that predates dance-band swing - no rural blues, and no bel canto either. He even sounds uncomfortable with a waltz.

So what? His extraordinary powers lay elsewhere, and he invented something else. He was the first at what he did, not the latest Crosby or Rudy Vallee. He didn't have the versatility of another great performer of his generation, Mel Torme, but he didn't need it. He was too busy ploughing his own fresh furrow. And in the setting of big-band swing - maybe with an additional curtain of strings, maybe pruned right back to its piano and rhythm section - he had all the material he needed.

In contrast to the 'Old Groaner' Crosby, Sinatra put great stress - literally - on clarity of diction. He enunciated the ends of words rather than chewed them off. This helped to give his work its intimate, conversational, even confessional character. On stage, this was bolstered by Sinatra's expert, indeed unprecedented, use of a hand-held microphone, to him the vocalist's instrument just as much as the piano was Count Basie's.

Sinatra dominated the scene for so long that it is easy to forget that his career might have lasted five years rather than 50. As a dance-band crooner in the Forties he provoked mass hysteria among his female audiences in a way that had never before been experienced in popular music, and was probably matched only by the scenes at the funeral of Rudolph Valentino.

And yet by the end of the decade it seemed for a while that his incandescent career might already have burned itself out. His record sales slumped in the early Fifties, his infatuation for Ava Gardner and tempestuous public affair with her, starting while he was still married to his first wife Nancy, cast him in an undignified light, and a new, melodramatic style of male vocalising came into vogue. Record-buyers could choose between the big-chested, Wild West declaiming of Frankie Laine and the pigeon-chested, hysterical pre-rock-'n'roll ballad style of Johnnie Ray, and in the meantime such fellow song stylists as Dick Haymes, Billy Eckstine and Perry Como were gaining ground. All this meant that, as we shall see later, he virtually had to pay Capitol to sign him to the contract that would triumphantly restore his reputation.

The problem was compounded when he was teamed with the new A&R man at Columbia, Mitch Miller, who showed little understanding of Sinatra's unique qualities. Famously, it took a film role - that of the GI Angelo Maggio in Fred Zinneman's 1953 success *From Here to Eternity* - to begin rebuilding his fortunes, an opportunity he had to do everything but go down on his knees to secure, but this was followed by far more sympathetic musical partners in the recording studio. He never looked back.

Sinatra's recording career falls into four broadly distinct chapters - his early days as a dance-band singer, the first years as a solo artist that took him to stardom and back again, his marvellous Fifties work on the Capitol label, and the decades on his own label, Reprise. There is a brief Nineties coda back on Capitol. All are fully represented on CD, and the purpose of this book is to provide a critical and chronological commentary on his recorded work, attempting to cut a logical path through the longest of all singing careers.

As such this is not a discography. This is not the place to provide, for example, a chronological list of every Sinatra 78 rpm single, because they are not available in that form. The bravest discographical enterprise regarding Sinatra's career that I am aware of is by William Ruhlmann in the May 3 1991 issue of the record junkie's bible *Goldmine*, a completists' compilation displaying terrier-like determination. This is instead a word picture of what you can go out and buy on CD today. In countries like the UK, where copyright protection lapses after 50 years, his early work is attracting the continuing attention of many independent labels, but every track should be in here somewhere. Whether you are tempted simply to replace a scratched copy of *Songs for Swingin' Lovers* or invest a Lottery win in the vast trunk packed with CD re-masters of his Reprise years, the material is featured in these pages.

Frank Sinatra enjoyed what is probably a uniquely long and productive career. This guide to his work on CD aims at completeness in surveying his officially-released work, together with numerous examples of 'public domain' material, collector's items from concerts, radio, television and studio out-takes, and out-and-out bootlegs. However, the Sinatra industry will roll on indefinitely, and his catalogue has already been re-permutated many times. Time, space and deadlines do not allow for every re-jigging of material already noted here in some form. This is particularly true of 'Best Of' and 'Greatest Hits' compilations and packages of what started life as singles. But they are easily available, and by definition the titles will tend to be more familiar than some of the material given greater coverage here. Wherever practical, track listings have been taken from CD sources. When this was not possible, such sources as session details, discographies and biographies were used, and this may result in slight running-order variations. In the age of digital remastering, sound quality of all official releases can be assumed to be excellent.

I have covered Sinatra's career chronologically from dance bands to dotage. After his early apprenticeship, the first significant stage was his decade as a solo singer recording for the Columbia label. This saw the phenomenon of Forties fan hysteria, and gradually demonstrated the emergence of the mature Sinatra style. (Since it may be less familiar to modern audiences than his later work I have given it, proportionately, somewhat greater attention). He then moved on to the revolutionary run of Capitol albums in the Fifties and in 1960 began his own record company, Reprise. Late in life he returned to Capitol. I have concluded this survey with a subjective selection of the key Sinatra CDs that could form the cornerstone of a basic collection.

John Collis, London, 1997

Acknowledgments

Most music journalists would agree that telephoning a major record company in search of information is a triumph of hope over experience, and so this book could not have been completed without the assistance of two Sinatra enthusiasts. Stan Britt, one of Frank Sinatra's biographers, kindly shared much of his knowledge, while John O'Toole of Charly Records gave me access to his record collection and library. My grateful thanks are due to both of them.

It would seem that if a British jazz journalist writes a pictorial biography of Sinatra, it must be called *Sinatra: a Celebration*. Stan Britt's (Hamlyn, 1995) was my constant companion, while other very useful 'celebrations' were written by Derek Jewell (Pavilion, 1985) and Ray Coleman (Pavilion, 1995). Fred Dellar, in writing *Sinatra: His Life and Times* (1995) for the company publishing this present work, chose a different and invaluable approach, by reconstructing Sinatra's life as a diary of events. For such information as session details, this was a huge help. Nancy Sinatra's *Frank Sinatra My Father* (Hodder and Stoughton, 1985) was also revealing. I consulted the *Official Price Guide to Frank Sinatra Records and CDs*, by Vito Marino and Anthony Furfero (House of Collectibles, 1993) and *Jazz and Blues Catalogue Edition 2*, edited by Graham Langley (Retail Entertainment Data, revised 1994).

The Dance Band Years

Frank Sinatra was born on 12 December 1915 in Hoboken, New Jersey, a charmless port across the Hudson River from New York City. His mother, Natalie Garavante, known to all as Dolly, came from Genoa and his father, Anthony Martin Sinatra, from Catania in Sicily. Although there was music in the family, probably the most valuable characteristic he inherited was his mother's determination and ambition, which saw her progress from organising petitions on behalf of the neighbourhood to working for the local Democratic Party organisation. As a result of these activities Dolly had little time for parenthood, and her only child grew up more in the company of his grandmother Rosa and a neighbour, Mrs Goldberg.

From his father the boy inherited an interest in boxing - Sinatra senior had once fought professionally as a bantamweight under the pugnacious Irish pseudonym Marty O'Brien, though by the time his son was born he was working in the shipyards as a boiler-maker, and soon progressed to the Fire Service. As numerous pressmen would later testify, the junior Sinatra's interest in pugilism did not always remain theoretical.

Francis Albert Sinatra grew up tough and street-wise, although the Sinatra home was far from being a slum. He ran with local street gangs and often got into fights. By his mid-teens he was clear in his own mind that he wanted to be a singer, an ambition probably prompted by the gift of a ukulele when he was 15. He left school early, half-heartedly signed up for a course in business administration, and during the Depression worked as a delivery boy for one of the local papers, the *Jersey Observer*. This, however, was simply to subsidise his attempts to impress local dance bands and club owners in his abilities as a crooner, and when at the age of 18 he went to a Bing Crosby concert in Jersey City, he knew beyond doubt that there was only one career for him.

By this time the family had prospered enough to buy their own home, at 841 Garden Street.

Frank's companion at the Crosby performance in 1934 was Nancy Barbato, who was to become his first wife four years later. Dolly relented in her opposition to the insecure world of the dance-band singer sufficiently to buy Frank his own portable PA system, which helped him in persuading bands to let him sit in with them. He also invested in a stock of sheet-music parts to distribute among the musicians. In 1935 he gained a brief residency at a local club, and later in the year joined vocal group the Hoboken Four, formerly the Three Flashes. In September they won a talent show, the Major Bowes Amateur Hour, which led to a gig at New York's Capitol Theater, and they were booked by Bowes to join his nation-wide touring roadshow. It was a break of sorts, but Frank soon fell out with his less talented partners, and left the tour.

By this time he had decided that the growing world of radio offered a better route to stardom, although for some while it meant offering to sing for nothing in order to build his reputation. He performed at a local social club, but left because it did not have the equipment necessary to link it to radio stations.

A more substantial break came in 1937 when Sinatra was hired by a road-house club, the Rustic Cabin, as a singing waiter. This teamed him with the resident Harold Arden Band, and the club had an all-important 'wire' to transmit its shows direct to radio station WNEW. Eventually this regular exposure did the trick and in 1939, soon after he married Nancy, one of Sinatra's regular weekly spots on WNEW's Dance Band Parade was heard by trumpeter and bandleader Harry James, a protégé of the great Benny Goodman. In June he came to the club especially to hear Sinatra, and signed him as his vocalist at $75 per week. This was three times his Rustic Cabin wage, and at the end of the month Sinatra quit his residency and joined the James band.

Such historical fragments of Sinatra's

pre-James career as exist are of curiosity value only, and 1935-1939: *The Beginnings and Harry James* includes a couple of Hoboken Four tracks and a private demo of a song called 'Our Love', while *The Rarest Sinatra* is a radio transcription from the show *Town Hall Tonight*.

"His name is Sinatra, and he considers himself the greatest vocalist in the business. Get that! No-one's even heard of him! He's never had a hit record, and he looks like a wet rag, but he says he's the greatest."

So said the usually benign Harry James to a journalist from *Down Beat* magazine about the cocky young singer he had just engaged. James, a virtuoso from Georgia whose trumpet style combined robust technique with unusual richness of tone, had formed his own band late in 1938 after a year or so with Benny Goodman, the King of Swing. He was in fact three months younger than Sinatra, and his rise to the top had been swift - youthful experience in his father's circus band, a move to play with the Ben

Pollack band in 1935 and then the brief stint with Goodman, who invested in the James outfit when his trumpeter expressed the wish to set up on his own.

This was the golden age of dance bands, a phenomenon whose growth had mirrored that of radio since the Twenties, and who were the major source of live music for the broadcast medium - a vital contribution, given the Musicians' Union's justifiable concern that an increased use of records on juke boxes and radio was a threat to musicians' livelihoods. This is where the 'wire' or 'remote' was essential, installed in all the most enterprising clubs and ballrooms to pump their music direct to late-night radio.

It was the Union who effectively ended the boom era for dance bands when they imposed a recording ban in 1942. But by this point Sinatra had already decided that his apprenticeship as a 'vocal refrain' was complete, and that he was ready to move on to the solo stage. It proved a well-timed decision.

James signed Sinatra to a two-year contract in June 1939, although the ambitious singer was to get itchy feet within six months. James imprudently suggested a name change to the manly moniker Frankie Satin, which was sternly resisted. Would we still be celebrating the work of a Mr Satin nearly six decades later?

When he talent-scouted Sinatra, James had a female singer in Connie Haines but no male lead, though trumpeter Jack Palmer filled the traditional role of comic and novelty vocalist. At the end of June, Sinatra appeared with the James band at the Hippodrome in Baltimore, singing 'My Love For You' and 'Wishing (Will Make It So)', before moving to New York's Roseland Ballroom for the remainder of the summer, where his 'pleasing vocals' and 'easy phrasing' gained him his first press notice. It was an intensive learning period, since the band also gigged at the World's Fair each afternoon.

Sinatra first entered a recording studio, to cut 'From the Bottom of My

Heart' and 'Melancholy Mood', on 13 July 1939. After the New York season the James band moved in October to Chicago's Sherman Hotel. A month later Tommy Dorsey's popular vocalist Jack Leonard left the Dorsey band to try his luck as a solo singer, to be replaced briefly by Allan DeWitt.

Sinatra featured in several Harry James sessions that autumn, but it took his later stardom for them to become belated hits, when re-released with the singer's name prominent. The most notable was 'All or Nothing At All', a comparative flop in 1939, a chart-topping gold disc in 1943.

After Chicago the band moved to Los Angeles to play at the Palomar, a club instrumental in launching Benny Goodman's career. But the building burned down when they were in transit, a hurried replacement booking failed, and they returned to Chicago in disarray.

This may well have prompted Sinatra's next move. Although he was only a quarter-way through his contract with Harry James, he was determined to land a job with the well-established and top-rated Dorsey outfit. He was also confident enough to audition with a number that was a highlight of Jack Leonard's repertoire, 'Marie', and it did the trick. Dorsey indicated that he was willing to improve Sinatra's wages once again.

James kindly decided not to balk Sinatra's ambitions, and tore up his contract. Sinatra would always remain grateful for this generosity, and has famously described his emotions after playing his last gig with the James band in January 1940, in Buffalo. "The bus pulled out with the rest of the boys at about half-past midnight. I'd said goodbye to them all and it was snowing. There was nobody around and I stood alone with my suitcase in the snow and watched the tail-lights disappear. Then the tears started and I tried to run after the bus..."

On 26 January Sinatra played his first Dorsey gig, in Rockford, Illinois, where he was given two solo numbers and earned an improvised encore. Whereas James, just starting up, had yet to attract star musicians, Sinatra now

FRANK WITH QUINCY JONES (LEFT) AND COUNT BASIE.

found himself working with such side-men as trumpeter Bunny Berigan and drummer Buddy Rich. Within a week he was recording with them, working with the arranger who was to shape his early career, Axel Stordahl, on 'The Sky Fell Down' and 'Too Romantic'. From then on, while with Dorsey, Sinatra was usually committed to two recording sessions every month.

The bandleader himself provided Sinatra with a lesson in technique - the singer noticed that the trombonist could play a lengthy legato sequence without seeming to pause for breath. This was because he had mastered a way of taking in air surreptitiously at the side of his mouth while maintaining the sequence of notes. As Sinatra's vocal style matured he translated this breath control into his own musical armoury, bolstered by fitness training and underwater swimming, giving him the ability to glide smoothly and expressively through extended passages of the lyric.

As well as taking his turn as a featured singer, Sinatra also blended in as part of the close-harmony ensemble within the band, The Pied Pipers, and as such contributed to Dorsey's huge 1940 hit 'I'll Never Smile Again', cut in New York in May. The pop charts as we came to know them only began in the early Fifties, but any system of computing record sales and popularity up until this time credits this as being one of the biggest of all pre-Hot Hundred hits. It established the Sinatra close-mike style, and confirmed him as the band's star vocalist. The song had been written by Ruth Lowe, and according to many accounts it was a reaction to her husband's death.

At the height of the dance-band phenomenon, as featured singer with one of the most popular of all the touring combos, Sinatra gained further concentrated apprenticeship from one-nighters and residencies, recording sessions and radio broadcasts, together with films like 1941's *Las Vegas Nights* and *Ship Ahoy*. He took full advantage of it, learning and advancing all the time. By the end of summer 1941 he felt ready to go it alone, and gave Dorsey a year's notice in September.

The following January, with Stordahl as arranger, he 'moonlighted' by cutting four solo sides with Dorsey's approval - the bandleader was still presumably hoping to keep his star. This session produced Sinatra's first solo hit, Cole Porter's 'Night and Day', and his last Dorsey session, 'Light a Candle in the Chapel', followed on 2 July 1942. Within a month the Union imposed its recording ban, and it lasted until late

1944. Although this effectively ended the dominance of the dance bands, singers could continue to record, solo or in harmony, as a cappella performers. Sinatra's timing proved immaculate.

HARRY JAMES AND HIS ORCHESTRA FEATURING FRANK SINATRA: THE COMPLETE RECORDINGS

From The Bottom of My Heart/ Melancholy Mood/ My Buddy/ It's Funny to Everyone But Me/ Here Comes the Night/ All or Nothing At All/ On a Little Street in Singapore/ Who Told You I Cared?/ Ciribiribin/ Every Day of My Life/ Stardust/ Wishing Will Make It So/ If I Don't Care/ The Lamp Is Low/ My Love For You/ Moon Love/ This Is No Dream

The historic first stage of Sinatra's career in full, with 'Frank Sinatra, vocals' as the last billing.

HARRY JAMES AND HIS ORCHESTRA FEATURING FRANK SINATRA: ALL OR NOTHING AT ALL

Ciribiribin/ My Buddy/ Avalon/ All Or Nothing At All/ Mean To Me/ Melancholy Mood/ I Found A New Baby/ From The Bottom Of My Heart/ Sweet Georgia Brown/ To You/ I Poured My Heart Into A Song/ The Japanese Sandman/ Here Comes The Night/ Undecided/ On A Little Street In Singapore/ Let's Disappear/ I'm Forever Blowing Bubbles

Sinatra does not feature on every track of this unofficial release on the Burbank label Hindsight, although he is on some of those not featured on the above official version.

DORSEY-SINATRA SESSIONS 1940-42

The Sky Fell Down/ Too Romantic/ Shake Down The Stars/ Moments In The Moonlight/ I'll Be Seeing You/ Say

It/ Polka Dots And Moonbeams/ The Fable Of The Rose/ This Is The Beginning Of The End/ Hear My Song Violetta/ Fools Rush In/ Devil May Care/ April Played The Fiddle/ I Haven't Time To Be A Millionaire/ Imagination/ Yours Is My Heart Alone/ You're Lonely And I'm Lonely/ East Of The Sun (And West Of The Moon)/ When You Awake/ Anything/ Shadows On The Sand/ You're Breaking My Heart All Over Again/ I'd Know You Anywhere/ Do You Know Why/ Not So Long Ago/ Stardust/ Oh Look At Me Now/ You Might Have Belonged To Another/ You Lucky People You/ It's Always You/ I Tried/ Dolores/ Without A Song/ Do I Worry/ Everything Happens To Me/ Let's Get Away From It All Parts 1 & 2/ I'll Never Let A Day Pass By/ Love Me As I Am/ This Love Of Mine/ I Guess I'll Have To Dream The Rest/ Free For All/ You And I/ Neiani/ Blue Skies/ Two In Love/ Violets For Your Furs/ Pale Moon/ I Think Of You/ How Do You Do Without Me/ A Sinner Kissed An Angel/ Violets For Your Furs/ The

RECORDING WITH COUNT BASIE.

Sunshine Of Your Smile/ How About You/ The Night We Called It A Day/ The Lamplighter's Serenade/ The Song Is You/ Night And Day/ Snootie Little Cutie/ Poor You/ I'll Take Tallulah/ The Last Call For Love/ Somewhere A Voice Is Calling/ Just As Though You Were Here/ Street Of Dreams/ Take Me/ Be Careful, It's My Heart/ In The Blue Of The Evening/ Dig Down Deep/ There Are Such Things/ Daybreak/ It Started All Over Again/ Light A Candle In The Chapel

From 1 February 1940 in Chicago to New York exactly 18 months later, usually as the featured singer but sometimes duetting with Connie Haines or as one of the Pied Pipers, Sinatra continued his concentrated apprenticeship in the studio. Many of these tracks were arranged by Axel Stordahl, who was to become the next big influence on Sinatra's career as his constant collaborator during the first solo decade.

TOMMY DORSEY/FRANK SINATRA ALL-TIME GREATEST HITS VOLUMES 1, 2 AND 3/THE HISTORICAL STORDAHL SESSIONS VOLUME 4

These four separate American CDs cover the same ground as the British Digipak above, and cover the two years Sinatra spent with Dorsey before going solo.

STARDUST

I'll Be Seeing You/ Polka Dots And Moonbeams/ Fools Rush In/ Imagination/ East Of The Sun (And West Of The Moon)/ I'll Never Smile Again/ Stardust/ Dolores/ This Love Of Mine/ Everything Happens To Me/ There Are Such Things

An 'official' American single-CD collection that represents the best of the Dorsey-Sinatra sides.

THIS ONE'S FOR TOMMY

I'll Never Smile Again/ Oh Look At Me Now/ This Love Of Mine/ Wrap Your Troubles In Dreams/ St Louis Blues (Jo Stafford)/ We Remember Tommy (Sinatra And Stafford)/ I'll Never Smile Again (Sinatra and Stafford)/ Dorsey Medley (Sinatra and Stafford)/ Our Love Is Here To Stay/ Dolores/ I'll Take Tallulah/ Whispering/ Without A Song/ I've Got A Restless Spell/ Is There A Chance For Me?/ Frenesi/ Let's Get Away From It All/ I Guess I'll Have To Dream The Rest/ Blue Skies/ Free For All

A historic and extensively researched 1995 compilation on the Voice imprint begins with the Sinatra-Dorsey reunion concert of 1955, continues with a TV tribute to Dorsey from 1958, with Jo Stafford as special guest and Nelson Riddle as arranger, adds a couple of film soundtrack recordings, and is completed by nine live rarities - taken by radio wire from hotel gigs - from the Dorsey-Sinatra period 1940/41.

TOMMY DORSEY AND HIS ORCHESTRA: 1942 WAR BOND BROADCAST

A collectors' item on Jazz Hour, also featuring Jo Stafford, Sinatra's rival Dick Haymes (who replaced Sinatra both with James and Dorsey) and with Ziggy Elman and Buddy Rich as the billed musicians in the band, this unearths a Treasury War Bond show on 19 July 1942, a Raleigh Cigarette show excerpt and a complete Haymes show.

THE FORMATIVE YEARS

Night And Day/ Oh! Look At Me Now/ How About You/ Fools Rush In/ Our Love Affair/ I Think Of You/ Imagination/ Whispering/ On A Little Street In Singapore/ All Or Nothing At All/ From The Bottom Of My Heart/ It's Funny To Everyone But Me/ Be Careful, It's My Heart/ I'll Be Seeing You/ It's Always You/ The Lamplighter's Serenade/ Stardust/ A Sinner Kissed An Angel/ Street Of Dreams/ This Love

Of Mine/ Let's Get Away From It All/ Everything Happens To Me/ This Is The Beginning Of The End/ The Song Is You

A very useful compilation by Stan Britt for the Avid label, in that on a single CD it picks plums from Sinatra's work with James, Dorsey and Stordahl. This is an example of those legal 'public domain' collections that exploit the 50-year copyright law in most countries. There are four tracks with James, 17 with Dorsey and the icing on the cake is the set of demos that Sinatra made with Stordahl when seeking a solo career.

THE KID FROM HOBOKEN (CHARLY)

Disc 1:
Stardust/ In The Blue Of The Evening/ All This And Heaven Too/ Pale Moon/ Moments In The Moonlight/ Anything/ Trade Winds/ Melancholy Mood/ The Sky Fell Down/ Not So Long Ago/ Shake Down The Stars/ Oh! What A Beautiful Morning/ The Fable Of The Rose/ Polka Dots And Moonbeams/

Looking For Yesterday/ Shadows On The Sand/ East Of The Sun/ The Night They Called It A Day/ Tell Me At Midnight/ April Played The Fiddle/ I Guess I'll Have To Dream The Rest/ Blue Skies

Disc 2:
Too Romantic/ The One I Love (Belongs To Somebody Else)/ From The Bottom Of My Heart/ Imagination/ You And I/ Fools Rush In/ Our Love Affair/ Take Me/ Close To You/ Street Of Dreams/ It's Always You/ Yours Is My Heart Alone/ I Could Make You Care/ People Will Say We're In Love/ Devil May Care/ Head On My Pillow/ Every Day Of My Life/ Be Careful, It's My Heart/ You Might Have Belonged To Another/ You'll Never Know/ I'd Know You Anywhere/ The Song Is You

Disc 3:
All Or Nothing At All/ Daybreak/ On A Little Street In Singapore/ There Are Such Things/ Poor You/ Say It/ Who

Told You I Cared?/ Just As Though You Were Here/ Do You Know Why/ You're Lonely And I'm Lonely/ It's A Lovely Day Tomorrow/ Ciribiribin/ Two In Love/ A Singer Kissed An Angel/ It's Funny To Everyone But Me/ The Call Of The Canyon/ The Last Call For Love/ Here Comes The Night/ Oh! Look At Me Now/ Without A Song/ Night And Day

Disc 4:
This Is The Beginning Of The End/ I'll Never Let A Day Pass/ Do I Worry?/ I'll Be Seeing You/ I Haven't Time To Be A Millionaire/ Where Do You Keep Your Heart?/ Love Me As I Am/ Let's Get Away From It All/ We Three/ How About You?/ Light A Candle In The Chapel/ This Love Of Mine/ I'll Never Smile Again/ Snootie Little Cutie/ Everything Happens To Me/ The Sunshine Of Your Smile/ How Do You Do Without Me?/ Violets For Your Furs/ Whispering/ You're

Breaking My Heart All Over Again/ The Lamplighter's Serenade

Of the independent record companies exploiting the early Sinatra catalogue in territories where copyright protection lapses after 50 years, Charly have the most extensive programme. It is pinned around this four-CD Digipak, useful in that it covers the Harry James/Tommy Dorsey period plus Sinatra's early years on Columbia as a solo singer. However, the sequence is not chronological - the source of each track is identified in the accompanying book insert - because the decision was taken to programme the tracks for listenability rather than historical development.

It should be remembered that as a dance-band employee Sinatra was simply a (usually anonymous) 'vocal refrain', entering the action towards the end of the tune for a few bars of glory. It was not until he found stardom as a solo singer on Columbia that re-issues of some of this material, notably the huge hit 'All or Nothing At All', promoted his name above the title.

Sinatra's voice had yet to acquire that burr of worldly wisdom - even world-weariness - that gave his mature work an extra edge. Also, within the discipline of the dance-band format, he could only begin to develop his unique ability in the legato technique of stretching a note as a wind instrument does. The talent is there, of course, but in embryonic form. Viewed as top-flight dance band singles of the day, however, these tracks come into their own, with the young Sinatra as a bonus.

Charly have also re-permutated this material in other ways. There are 45 tracks on the double set *The Romantic Sinatra*, which draws on material up to and including 1945. *Young Blue Eyes* is a very useful introduction to early Sinatra, as its 25 tracks include solo work, two

Harry James tracks, nine with Tommy Dorsey and five radio transcriptions, together with an informative booklet note by Stan Britt. A further 25-tracker, *Among My Souvenirs*, is a general selection, and Charly's exploitation of the catalogue to date is completed by the more specific *The Dorsey Years*, 20 tracks that sum up Sinatra's period with the Tommy Dorsey band.

As you can see, it is possible to match your degree of Sinatraphilia to the amount of material you collect from his early career - the whole caboodle on official releases, the four-CD Charly compilation or the single CD *The Formative Years* are perhaps the most obvious staging posts.

WITH PEGGY LEE AND BING CROSBY.

The Columbia Years

Tommy Dorsey was not as generous as Harry James had been when negotiating Sinatra's release. He demanded a third of the singer's gross earnings for ten years, with another ten per cent for his manager. Eventually, in August 1943 after protracted legal wrangling, Sinatra's agency MCA bought out Dorsey's interest in a package worth over $100,000.

There was logic in the fact that Sinatra the solo singer should sign to the recently revived Columbia label. The newly appointed head of A&R, Manny Sachs, knew and liked his work, and indeed the singles recorded with the Harry James band were in Columbia's catalogue. Furthermore, Sinatra had sent acetates of his January solo recordings to Sachs, who led him to understand that a contract would be forthcoming when he was a free agent. And so, in September 1942, Sinatra left Dorsey and took Stordahl with him. The ban on musicians being involved in recording sessions had just come into force. Sinatra's first move was to investigate Hollywood, but the only fruit was a cameo performance in a musical revue, *Reveille With Beverly*.

It was clear that the gamble had paid off, however, when Sinatra appeared in concert at the Paramount Theater in New York. He was a 'special added attraction' on a bill topped by the Benny Goodman Orchestra, opening on 30 December for a month's run. A journalist dubbed the resulting phenomenon 'Sinatrauma', with a huge crowd of screaming, hysterical teenage girls fighting to get into the theatre and stopping the traffic for blocks around. Both Goodman and Sinatra were taken aback at the force of the fan reaction, but only Sinatra was pleased by it. As they stood behind the curtain and became aware of the uproar, one reported reaction of the King of Swing was to say in an astonished tone of voice: 'What the fuck is that?' After that, they were billed as co-stars, and Sinatra had his run extended for a further month as the main attraction.

Suddenly, everything started happening for him. His radio show was launched in February 1943, his first night-club season, at New York's Riobamba Club, began a month later - the run was extended twice, with Sinatra's weekly wage starting at $750 and ending at double that. In May he returned to the Paramount, and in August he starred at the Hollywood Bowl.

This marked the conclusion of a tour with the Los Angeles Philharmonic Orchestra. The partnership, and the fact that a mere crooner had been allowed to step out into the Hollywood Bowl, had drawn unfavourable comments from some intellectually élitist quarters, and the young Sinatra displayed a character-istic willingness to use the stage as a lecture platform.

"I'd just like to say thank you from the bottom of my heart," he said. "There's been quite a controversy out here as to whether or not I should appear here at the Bowl, and I want to say that it seems as though those people who thought I shouldn't kind of lost out in a very big way. I have a comment to make about that - I don't see why there shouldn't be a mixture of all kinds of music in any bowl or in any public auditorium. Music is uni-versal, whether you hear a concert singer with a philharmonic orchestra or a crooner with a jazz band, it doesn't make any difference."

His first a cappella sessions took place in the second half of the year, but in the meantime, in spite of the Union ban, re-issues of his dance-band recordings kept Sinatra in the charts.

'Sinatrauma' reached its height when, in October 1944, he starred once more at the Paramount. On the first day all seats were occupied by early morning, and on the second, in what came to be dubbed the Columbus Day Riot, Times Square was blocked and New York experienced new heights of hysteria and mayhem. This was all orchestrated by Sinatra's highly skilled press agent, George Evans.

For most of the decade Sinatra remained at the height of his popularity on all fronts. He had yet to find a truly memorable movie role, it is true, but his semi-autobiographical appearances kept the fans happy. His radio shows remained popular, and he continued to gain in stature both as a live performer and, as we shall see, as a recording artist - he seemed to be pioneering the concept of using the studio to create an art form in itself, rather than seeing records simply as portable and marketable souvenirs of a popular artist.

By the end of the decade, however, it seemed that this extraordinary career might be over, for the reasons outlined in the introductory chapter. Had Sinatra indeed faded away as a commercial force, he had already created an impressive enough recorded legacy to be judged by music history to be one of the greats - and this without the Capitol masterpieces, the huge Reprise hits like 'My Way', and without ol' blue eyes ever coming back.

THE COLUMBIA YEARS 1943-1952 - THE COMPLETE RECORDINGS
(COLUMBIA LEGACY)

A sumptuous 12-CD set complete with 144-page book, session and release details. It is complete in the sense that every Columbia track is included, but we are spared false starts and too many alternate takes. Any duplication of titles has some illustrative purpose, besides the fact that Sinatra often returned to a song, like 'White Christmas' or 'Nancy (With the Laughing Face)', to interpret it anew.

Disc 1:
Close To You/ You'll Never Know/ Sunday, Monday Or Always/ If You Please/ People Will Say We're In Love/ Oh, What A Beautiful Mornin'/ I Couldn't Sleep A Wink Last Night/ A Lovely Way To Spend An Evening/ The Music Stopped/ If You Are But A Dream/ Saturday Night (Is The

Loneliest Night Of The Week)/ There's No You/ White Christmas/ I Dream Of You (More Than You Dream Of Me)/ I Begged Her/ What Makes The Sunset?/ I Fall In Love Too Easily/ Nancy (With The Laughing Face)/ Cradle Song/ Ol' Man River/ Stormy Weather/ The Charm Of You

Sinatra was almost a year into his Columbia contract before he entered a recording studio. No-one had expected the Union ban on their members taking part in recording sessions to last this long, and though he was no doubt impatient to see his name on a solo record, there was plenty of work to do on radio and the stage, including the sensational Paramount run beginning in December 1942, while re-issues of his dance-band work at least kept his name in the record racks, notably via the major hit 1939 Harry James title 'All or Nothing At All'.

The idea of recording without instruments was resisted for as long as possible, but with no sign of the Union giving in (or being forced to by Congress)

WITH BARBARA RUSH IN *COME BLOW YOUR HORN*.

Sinatra went into the studio on 7 June 1943 to cut 'Close To You' and 'You'll Never Know'. By August both sides of the disc were in the Top Ten. They were the first of nine a cappella sides cut between June and November, with arrangements by Alec Wilder and backing by the Bobby Tucker Singers, who varied in number between nine and 17.

'Close To You', Sinatra's historic first cut as a solo star, set the pattern, with Wilder scoring for voices as if for an orchestra, and the young singer, though yet to acquire the 'burr' in his voice that gave his mature work so much of its force, sounding totally confident and in command of the microphone. On the flip-side, the voices are often required to ape string patterns. Wilder, nicknamed 'The Professor' by Sinatra, was preferred as vocal arranger over the singers' leader Bobby Tucker, and commanded a group that included two celebrated musical directors of the future in 'the other' Ray Charles and Norman Luboff. Wilder's job, of course, was to solve an impossible problem - to replace instruments with voices without anyone noticing, or objecting.

The fact that seven of the nine titles charted may be a vindication of the a cappella exercise, or simply a measure of the singer's extraordinary appeal at the time. It must be admitted that one can often almost hear the concentration as everyone strains to pitch everything as intended, and some of the choices are strange - in particular the perennial thigh-slapper from Rodgers and Hammerstein's *Oklahoma*, 'Oh, What a Beautiful Mornin'', which sounds a bit like a vocal exercise. Far more successful and suitable is the confidential, confessional nature of 'I Couldn't Sleep a Wink Last Night', a genuinely touching piece of work. After cutting nine titles, however (more than any of the other strike-bound vocalists of the day) enough was clearly considered to be enough, and Sachs and Sinatra sat out a further year of the strike without returning to the studio.

On 14 November 1944, within three days of the Union and Columbia settling their differences, Sinatra resumed his partnership with Axel Stordahl and cut four tracks. As if celebrating their renewed access to musicians in the studio, Stordahl assembled a full orchestra including 18 string players, and the first song 'If You Are But a Dream' shows their fully-fledged collaborative sound. 'Saturday Night', the first Columbia cut by Sinatra's most consistent writing team Jule Styne and Sammy Cahn, was the up-tempo swinger of the four, while the inevitable 'White Christmas' was a hit for Sinatra both that Christmas and the next. Although we have seen that he deliberately moulded his technique to be clearly distinct from that of Crosby, there is more than a touch of the Old Groaner's pipe-and-comfy-shoes style in Sinatra's reading.

Everyone, including Styne and Cahn, was back on 1 December for a quartet of songs, assuring Sinatra of two further hits in the first half of 1945. A booting version of the *Anchors Aweigh* tune 'I Begged Her', though lacking the film's Gene Kelly, is the day's standout, with

Sinatra holding the word 'I' for as long as he dares. Two days later the final five songs on disc 1 were recorded, including a previously-unreleased attempt at a song that stayed with Sinatra throughout his career, 'Nancy (With the Laughing Face)', with lyrics by future Sgt Bilko, Phil Silvers. He is not entirely comfortable with the blue notes of 'Stormy Weather', though it is an intriguing attempt, as is the version of a song already a regular part of his repertoire, 'Ol' Man River'. It may be that the song will always remain in the firm grasp of Paul Robeson, but Sinatra's version of the song holds far more technical ingenuity than the original did.

Disc 2:

Embraceable You/ When Your Lover Has Gone/ Kiss Me Again/ (I Got A Woman Crazy For Me) She's Funny That Way/ My Melancholy Baby/ Where Or When/ All The Things You Are/Mighty Lak' A Rose/ I Should Care/ Homesick - That's All/ Dream (When You're Feeling Blue)/ A Friend

Of Yours/ Put Your Dreams Away (For Another Day)/ Over The Rainbow/ You'll Never Walk Alone/ If I Loved You/ Lily Belle/ Don't Forget Tonight Tomorrow/ I've Got A Home In That Rock/ Jesus Is A Rock In The Weary Land/ Stars In Your Eyes/ My Shawl

On 19 December 1944 Sinatra and Stordahl were back in the studio in Hollywood to cut four titles. The first, second and fourth tracks on this CD were to be re-recorded by Sinatra during his Capitol years, and the Gershwin standard 'Embraceable You', in particular, has been associated with him ever since. On 29 January 1945 he cut a pared-down version of a song until then the 'property' of Crosby, 'My Melancholy Baby'. Rodgers and Hart's 'Where or When', with effective contributions from the nine-strong Ken Lane Singers, has caught the attention of a variety of singers over the years, including doo-wop rockers Dion and The Belmonts, polite harmony group The Lettermen and Welsh rock 'n' roll legend Dave Edmunds - a wide compass.

Kern and Hammerstein's 'All the Things You Are' has proved similarly popular, and Sinatra's rich-textured version here is distinguished by what is, for him, a rare 'big finish'. The session was completed by a 1901 chestnut 'Mighty Lak' a Rose', which demonstrates Sinatra's art in taking obscure and even ordinary material and finding something of interest lurking within the song.

The pattern of the four-song session was repeated on 6 March. 'I Should Care' adds a Cahn lyric to a tune by Stordahl and Paul Weston, and it is noticeable that Sinatra approaches the title phrase from a slightly different angle each time - a text-book demonstration of his ability to illuminate a lyric probably more than even the writer realised was possible.

Other points of interest from this day's work: 'Homesick - That's All' was written by one of Sinatra's great collaborators of later years, Gordon Jenkins; Johnny Mercer's 'Dream' marked a return to a standard from the Dorsey days; and 'A Friend of Yours' featured in the movie *The Great John L*, which involved débutant producer Bing Crosby.

Four more titles followed on 1 May including a version of Sinatra's radio-show closer 'Put Your Dreams Away' by the enigmatic writer of 'I'll Never Smile Again', Ruth Lowe - he re-cut it both for Capitol and for his own label Reprise. On 'Over the Rainbow' he does not go out of his way to avoid comparison with Judy Garland, but still creates something of his own - though, perhaps blasphemously, I insist on a preference for the version of this sentimental war-horse by rocker Gene Vincent, a Capitol label-mate of Sinatra's in the Fifties. It seems doubtful that The Voice and Crazy Legs were ever to be spotted comparing notes on the song in the Capitol Tower canteen, however.

The usual cod opera of 'You'll Never Walk Alone' and 'If I Loved You' from Carousel is abandoned as, once again, Sinatra finds the unexpected in the familiar. In this case, he rejects the usual

impersonal bombast of these songs and turns them into something individual and intimate.

It may seem churlish to be less than delighted when Sinatra tries something markedly different, as he did during two further sessions of May 1945, but the results do seem to have more historic and curiosity value than great musical worth. He first cut four numbers with gospel group The Charioteers, who had also worked with Crosby, and a classy small band including trumpeter Red Nichols, with two straight gospel songs included on the menu. There are of course many delights here, above all some arresting vocal harmonies, but Sinatra is no gospel singer, and 'I've Got a Home in that Rock' stubbornly refuses to roll.

Later in the month he recorded with Spanish-born Cuban bandleader Xavier Cugat, and while the rhumba 'Stars in your Eyes' has its many charms, it is difficult to take seriously any song with the title 'My Shawl', even if it is a version of the distinguished Cugat's theme tune.

Disc 3:

Someone To Watch Over Me/ You Go To My Head/ These Foolish Things (Remind Me Of You)/ I Don't Know Why (I Just Do)/ The House I Live In (That's America To Me)/ Day By Day/ Nancy (With The Laughing Face)/ You Are Too Beautiful/ America The Beautiful/ Silent Night, Holy Night/ The Moon Was Yellow (And The Night Was Young)/ I Only Have Eyes For You/ The Old School Teacher/ Just An Old Stone House/ Full Moon And Empty Arms/ Oh, What It Seemed To Be/ I Have But One Heart (O Marenariello)/ (I Don't Stand) A Ghost Of A Chance/ Why Shouldn't I?/ Try A Little Tenderness/ Paradise/ All Through The Day/ One Love/ Two Hearts Are Better Than One/ How Cute Can You Be?

Sinatra's next recording session with Stordahl, on 30 July 1945, was a landmark in his career since it contributed the first four songs to what became his first 'concept' album, *The Voice*. This eight-tracker was also the first original

album by a popular singer. Instrumentation was pared back to a four-piece string section over a bass/drums/piano/guitar rhythm section, with guitar often establishing the feel of the song, and a ninth instrument was added for detail - a bird-like flute at this first session, an oboe when the album was completed in December.

Mood, tempo and arrangements were given a consistency of approach, and Sinatra tackled the selection as being of a piece. He was relaxed, in control of the material, deceptively at ease. When he returned to the project on 7 December he began with 'A Ghost of a Chance', with its opening line: 'I need your love so badly...'. One can detect the very kernel of his appeal to a young, female audience here, and it seems to be the key to this pioneering album. One can almost hear him transferring the natural habitat of the vinyl disc from the juke box to the private room.

Another of the December cuts was also taken from the Bing Crosby songbook along with 'Ghost...', though these days 'Try a Little Tenderness' may more often be associated with the singer who epitomised deep Southern soul in the Sixties, Otis Redding. But where Redding treated the song as would a preacher giving a little marriage guidance from a storefront pulpit, Sinatra is confiding advice to a close friend. This is totally in keeping with the intimate, chamber feel that he and Stordahl brought to *The Voice*, which after its initial 1945 release has not subsequently been presented in the intended form.

There were four other sessions in late 1945, however, and we should now backtrack to another key record that was a result of a session on August 22. 'What is America to me?' asks Sinatra in 'The House I Live In'. 'A name, a map, a flag?... democracy!... All races and religions, that's America to me.' Sinatra was later, of course, to consort with such liberal humanitarians as Nixon and Agnew, but in 1945 he was a powerful crusader for tolerance, a one-man campaign against bigotry. The song was written by Lewis Allen (who gave Billie

Holiday her most chilling political statement, 'Strange Fruit') and Earl Robinson, whose other political compositions included 'Black and White'. Sinatra turned the song into an Oscar-winning short film as well.

The session also took him back to the Phil Silvers/Jimmy Van Heusen song that he had featured many times on radio and recorded a year earlier in a then-unreleased version, 'Nancy (With the laughing Face)', which became a mainstay of his repertoire. Together with two coolly observed love songs, 'Day By Day' and 'You Are Too Beautiful', this day's work produced three chart entries.

If it's August 27 it must be Christmas, and so Sinatra cut 'Silent Night' with a full orchestra and the Ken Lane singers, 12 in number this time. He also celebrated the Allied victory - and offset 'The House I Live In' - by recording 'America the Beautiful', but it is noticeable that he avoids bombast and blind patriotism, stressing instead the optimism of the lyric. 'The Moon Is Yellow',

one of three Sinatra recordings of this song, shows him handling the tango rhythm by ignoring it, and the session was completed by a lush return to 'I Only Have Eyes For You'.

A curious session on November 15 teamed Sinatra with oboist, writer and arranger Alec Wilder and Columbia A&R man Mitch Miller for 'The Old School Teacher' and 'Just an Old Stone House', both somewhat undistinguished slices of nostalgia. On November 30 it was back to Stordahl and a cascade of strings - three songs, three hits, notably 'Oh, What It Seemed To Be'.

After completing *The Voice* in December Sinatra returned to the studio on February 3 1946 for a split session with Stordahl, cutting two songs with his customary full orchestra and two with a jumpier jazz line-up. The last two, 'Two Hearts Are Better Than One' and 'How Cute Can You Be?', bring a welcome change of tempo to this particular CD, and are distinguished by the nimble guitar work of Dave Barbour.

Disc 4:
From This Day Forward/ Where Is My Bess?/ Begin The Beguine/ Something Old, Something New/ They Say It's Wonderful/ That Old Black Magic/ The Girl That I Marry/ I Fall In Love With You Ev'ry Day/ How Deep Is The Ocean (How Blue Is The Sky)/ Home On The Range/ The Song Is You/ Soliloquy (Parts 1 & 2)/ Somewhere In The Night/ Could'ja?/ Five Minutes More/ The Things We Did Last Summer/ You'll Know When It Happens/ This Is The Night/ The Coffee Song (They've Got An Awful Lot Of Coffee In Brazil)/ Among My Souvenirs/ I Love You/ September Song/ Blue Skies/ Guess I'll Hang My Tears Out To Dry

On 24 February 1946 Sinatra, Stordahl and the customary full orchestra re-assembled in Hollywood for 'From This Day Forward' with its notable legato phrasing; the Gershwin show tune 'Where Is My Bess?', its meaning limited out of context; an effortless ride through 'Begin the Beguine'; and the

brazen seduction of 'Something Old...', with a sweet-toned Sinatra supported by a sensuous Herbie Haymer sax break.

The session on March 10 tackled an almost unprecedented seven songs, with the Irving Berlin *Annie Get Your Gun* numbers 'They Say It's Wonderful' and 'The Girl That I Marry' continuing the run of hits. Other highlights were a subtly swinging 'That Old Black Magic' and a further Berlin song, 'How Deep Is The Ocean...', to which Stordahl's arrangement brings a frisson of drama to the lovelorn hyperbole of the lyric. The Crosby-style corn of 'Home on the Range' provided a strange contrast.

The May 28 session was highlighted by a massive piece of work, Rodgers and Hammerstein's epic 'Soliloquy' from *Carousel*, describing a father's hopes for his unborn son (with the melody dropping into a minor key to face the unthinkable - that the baby might turn out to be... ahem... a girl!) Columbia spread this over both sides of a 12" disc. Taken as a technical exercise alone, it is a stunning performance.

The lush smooch of 'Somewhere in the Night' followed, before the orchestra was pared down to its jazz core for 'Could'Ja?', reuniting Sinatra with the rest of Dorsey's Pied Pipers; and a jaunty 'Five Minutes More'.

Among the sides cut on July 24 were the risqué seduction story of 'This Is the Night' and, in contrast, Sinatra's celebrated 'The Coffee Song', showing him far more at home with Latin rhythms than hitherto. The CD concludes with the five tracks from another successful day's work on 30 July, notably the perfectly realised melancholy of 'Among My Souvenirs', here in a previously unreleased take; Sinatra the 30-year old tackling Kurt Weill's 'September Song'; a cracking 'Blue Skies'; and the Styne/Cahn lament he'd return to on *Only the Lonely*, 'Guess I'll Hang My Tears Out to Dry'.

Disc 5:

Adeste Fideles (O, Come All Ye Faithful)/ Lost In The Stars/ Jingle Bells/ Falling In Love With Love/ Hush-A-Bye Island/ So They Tell Me/ There's No Business Like Show Business/ (Once Upon) A Moonlight Night/ Strange Music/ Poinciana (Song Of The Tree)/ The Music Stopped/ Why Shouldn't It Happen To Us/ Time After Time/ It's The Same Old Dream/ I'm Sorry I Made You Cry/ None But The Lonely Heart/ The Brooklyn Bridge/ I Believe/ I Got A Gal I Love (In North And South Dakota)/ The Dum-Dot Song (I Put A Penny In The Gum Slot)/

All Of Me/ It's All Up To You/ My Romance

On 8 August Sinatra returned to Kurt Weill for the complex 'Lost in the Stars' and clocked up his Christmas contributions, an unadorned 'Adeste Fideles' and an undistinguished 'Jingle Bells' (hardly Sinatra fodder), as well as a lively first look at Rodgers and Hart's 'Falling in Love with Love'. His form faltered for the next two sessions, on 22 August and 15 October, and half the tracks were left on the shelf until this collection. From the silly lullaby 'Hush-a-Bye Island' to the charming but lightweight 'Why Shouldn't It Happen To Us', he remained muted.

On 24 October he bounced back with a vengeance in Styne/Cahn's stunning 'Time After Time', a revealing demonstration of Sinatra's inexhaustible lungs. A week later he cut his first version of the Tchaikovsky adaptation 'None But the Lonely Heart' - one of the many worthy songs of the day, I confess, that we fans of Spike Jones and his City

Slickers find it hard to take seriously. Staying with Styne and Cahn, Sinatra turned 'The Brooklyn Bridge' into a convincing urban poem, swung nimbly into the big hit of the session 'I Believe' and charmed his way through 'I Got a Gal I Love', though Cahn's delight in his 'Dakota/iota/quota' rhymes are a touch transparent.

On 7 November Sinatra stumbled by electing to record the ridiculous 'Dum-Dot Song', before ripping into George Siravo's arrangement of 'All Of Me' - a top-notch up-tempo achievement. For the rest of the session he duetted with chum Dinah Shore for the first time in the studio, but the results stayed in the can - though a later version of 'My Romance' would soon be released.

Disc 6:
Always/ I Want To Thank Your Folks/ That's How Much I Love You/ You Can Take My Word For It Baby/ Sweet Lorraine/ Always/ I Concentrate On You/ My Love For You/ Mam'selle/ Ain'tcha Ever Comin' Back/ Stella By Starlight/ There But For You Go I/ Almost Like Being In Love/ Tea For Two/ My Romance/ Have Yourself A Merry Little Christmas/ Christmas Dreaming (A Little Early This Year)/ The Stars Will Remember (So Will I)/ It All Came True/ That Old Feeling/ If I Had You/ The Nearness Of You/ One For My Baby (And One More For The Road)

On 15 December 1946, after a laid-back, confiding version of Irving Berlin's 'Always' and the lesser romance of 'I Want to Thank Your Folks', Sinatra sent the orchestra home and swung into small-combo jazz with the Page Cavanaugh Trio, thought of at the time as a white version of the more celebrated Nat 'King' Cole Trio. Guitarist Al Viola would later become a permanent Sinatra collaborator, and here helps 'That's How Much I Love You' and 'You Can Take My Word For It Baby' stand out from the more familiar Stordahl strings.

The logical, and historic, next step occurred on 17 December, when Nat 'King' Cole himself swung into Sinatra's

LEFT TO RIGHT: MILTON BERLE, FRANK AND SAMMY DAVIS JNR.

reading of 'Sweet Lorraine' - a number Cole had made his own. The session also brought together drummer Buddy Rich and trumpeter Charlie Shavers from Sinatra's Dorsey days, Laurence Brown, Johnny Hodges, Coleman Hawkins and Harry Carney - a mouth-watering line-up.

On 9 January 1947 Sinatra made a

swift return to 'Always' and added a gently bouncing version of Cole Porter's 'I Concentrate On You' as well as the forgettable 'My Love for You'. His next visit to the studio, on 11 March, scored three hits out of three - the chart-topping romance of 'Mam'selle', the charming Stordahl/Pied Pipers collaboration

'Ain'tcha Ever Comin' Back' and the mysterious 'Stella By Starlight'.

Twenty days later Sinatra cut outstanding versions of two Brigadoon songs, his beautiful 'Almost Like Being in Love' continuing the chart run, before being reunited with Dinah Shore on 25 April for lightweight readings of 'Tea for Two' and 'My Romance'. And Christmas arrived even earlier than usual in 1947 - 3 July - and 'Christmas Dreaming' proved to be the seasonal hit. The bluesy 'The Stars Will Remember' and an unreleased but strong version of the up-tempo 'It All Came True' (a September re-cut was preferred) completed the day.

This sixth CD ends with a 'chamber' session - four-piece rhythm and just four strings - very much in the style of the tracks that had made up the album *The Voice*. Notable is a first visit to the Harold Arlen/Johnny Mercer classic 'One For My Baby' which, when re-recorded in 1958, defined the Sinatra persona of the period.

Disc 7:

But Beautiful/ A Fellow Needs A Girl/ So Far/ It All Came True/ Can't You Just See Yourself?/ You're My Girl/ All Of Me/ I'll Make Up For Ev'rything/ Strange Music/ Laura/ Night And Day/ My Cousin Louella/ We Just Couldn't Say Goodbye/ S'posin'/ Just For Now/ None But The Lonely Heart/ The Night We Called It A Day/ The Song Is You/ What'll I Do?/ Poinciana (Song Of The Tree)/ (I Offer You The Moon) Señorita/ The Music Stopped

Sinatra cut three more hits on 17 August 1947 - the understated Crosby vehicle 'But Beautiful' and two current Rodgers and Hammerstein show tunes from *Allegro*, here presented in previously unreleased takes. 'A Fellow Needs a Girl' is standard musical fare but 'So Far' is an outstanding love song, tenderly treated.

A one-song session on 23 September is an oddity, with Sinatra backed on 'It All Came True' by a six-piece hotel jazz combo led by Alvy West.

On 19 October it was back to the full orchestra for two songs from a new Styne/Cahn musical *High Button Shoes*. 'Can't You Just See Yourself' sounds like a song rejected for *Oklahoma* as being too corny, but 'You're My Girl' fares much better. The day's highlight, though, was the George Siravo arrangement of 'All of Me', built on an intriguing piano figure by Ken Lane - a palpable hit.

Sinatra was now entering the studio every couple of days, because another musicians' strike was threatened. On 22 October, with Stordahl and the trademark full orchestra, Sinatra produced a lush 'I'll Make Up For Ev'rything', a return to the score of *Song of Norway* for 'Strange Music', a suitably ethereal 'Laura' and a new version of the Cole Porter classic 'Night and Day'. The song had long been associated with Sinatra - he first recorded it in 1942 and opened his radio show with it - but this striking version unaccountably remained on the shelf.

Another welcome break from Stordahl's waterfall of violins came two days later, when Sinatra cut three easy-swinging numbers with a jazz trio - guitarist Tony Mottola, who was to rejoin Sinatra's road band in the 1980s, pianist and arranger John Guarnieri, and bassist Herman Alpert. 'My Cousin Louella' is a silly song but the attractive 'We Just Couldn't Say Goodbye' and the light-weight charm of 'S'posin'' made up for it. Guarnieri swapped piano for a delicate celeste figure in the middle number.

Back with the full, lush orchestra 48 hours later, Sinatra revisited the Tchaikovsky steal 'None But The Lonely Heart' in a 'big' version; the melancholy 'The Night We Called It A Day', also tackled in 1942 and 1957; and another Sinatra standby 'The Song Is You'; together with a confident reading of a then-current favourite 'Just For Now'.

Three days later Sinatra cut a masterly version of Irving Berlin's affecting 'What'll I Do?', familiar in Britain today as the theme tune of the hugely successful sitcom *Birds of a Feather*. Equally strong was a return to one of the songs he recorded during the musicians' ban at the start of his solo career, the dramatic 'The Music Stopped'. Sinatra also dabbled in Latin exotica, re-recording 'Poinciana' and adding a new song, 'Señorita'.

Disc 8:

Mean To Me/ Spring Is Here/ Fools Rush In (Where Angels Fear To Tread)/ When You Awake/ It Never Entered My Mind/ I've Got A Crush On You/ Body And Soul/ I'm Glad There Is You/ I Went Down To Virginia/ If I Only Had A Match/ If I Steal A Kiss/ Autumn In New York/ Everybody Loves Somebody/ A Little Learnin' Is A Dangerous Thing, Part 1/ A Little Learnin' Is A Dangerous Thing, Part 2/ Ever Homeward/ But None Like You/ Catana/ Why Was I Born?/ It Came Upon A Midnight Clear/ O Little Town Of Bethlehem/ White Christmas/ For Every Man There's A Woman

On 31 October and 5 November 1947 Sinatra and Stordahl worked on the LP follow-up to *The Voice*, to be called *Frankly Sentimental*. They began once more with a pared-down orchestra of four strings, wind and rhythm. Chris Griffin's trumpet is to the fore on a relaxed 'Mean to Me', to be replaced by Mitch Miller's oboe on the melancholy 'Spring Is Here' and a mature return to a Dorsey choice, 'Fools Rush In'.

On the next session the solo star is the great trumpeter Bobby Hackett. Sinatra revives another number from the Dorsey days, the smooth romance of 'When You Awake'; displays his distinctively intimate microphone technique on 'It Never Entered My Mind'; and scores a hit with the Gershwins' 'I've Got a Crush on You', kicked off by Hackett.

The latter was back, now in the company of a full orchestra, four days later for an outstanding two-song date - the Billie Holiday feature 'Body and Soul' sports a virtuoso trumpet solo, and Sinatra is in masterly control of both this and the smoothly romantic 'I'm Glad There Is You', formerly associated with Bob Eberle.

On 25 November Sinatra fronted a jaunty line-up featuring ten brass players with no strings attached, bouncing enjoyably through 'I Went Down to Virginia', but the day's other chore, 'If I Only Had a Match', fails to catch fire. Somewhere within it, though, is another preliminary drawing for the singer's 'loner' persona of later years.

The full Stordahl treatment was reinstated on 4 December for an undistinguished, vaguely Latin, 'If I Steal a Kiss'; a smooth treatment of a song that became pal Dean Martin's theme, 'Everybody Loves Somebody'; and a dramatic, atmospheric urban masterpiece, 'Autumn in New York'.

The idea of a black and a white star sharing a jokey duet was too startling for 'A Little Learning is a Dangerous Thing', cut on 8 December, to be a success; the material is stretched too far, perhaps, over two sides of a 78; and Sinatra is still no blues singer, and yet this rap with Pearl Bailey, arranged by Sy Oliver for a jazz septet, now sounds a sheer delight. It is unlike anything Sinatra had done before, Bailey is a far stronger performer than Dinah Shore,

and there seems to be a genuine rapport lurking behind the somewhat arch dialogue. It is a huge contrast to the weak sentimentality of the day's other cut, Styne/Cahn's 'Ever Homeward'.

The stockpiling of material at this time continued at a Boxing Day session, but they needn't have interrupted their holiday - it produced an undistinguished Ray Noble ballad, 'But None Like You', and the listless, uncertainly-pitched 'Catana'. And whereas Sinatra's thoughts usually turned to Christmas in the summer, he returned on 28 December with the Ken Lane Singers for respectful versions of 'It Came Upon a Midnight Clear' and 'O Little Town of Bethlehem' as well as a revisit to 'White Christmas' that adds nothing to his earlier version. 'Why Was I Born' is a sweet-toned Kern/Hammerstein number, and the CD ends with the dramatic, complex 'For Every Man There's a Woman'.

Disc 9:
Help Yourself To My Heart/ Santa Claus Is Coming To Town/ If I Forget You/

FRANK WITH BING CROSBY AND DOROTHY LAMOUR.

Where Is The One?/ When Is Sometime?/ It Only Happens When I Dance With You/ A Fella With An Umbrella/ Nature Boy/ Sunflower/ Once In Love With Amy/ Why Can't You Behave?/ Bop! Goes My Heart/ Comme Çi, Comme Ça/ No Orchids For My Lady/ While The Angelus Was Ringing (Les Trois Cloches)/ If You Stub Your Toe On The Moon/ Kisses And Tears/ Some Enchanted Evening/ Bali Ha'i/The Right Girl For Me/ Night After Night/ The Huckle-Buck/ It Happens Every Spring

This CD begins by completing the 28 December session with an effective smooch number 'Help Yourself To My Heart' and a bright 'Santa Claus Is Coming to Town'. But the stockpiling continued three days later - the new studio ban was due on the stroke of New Year, and favoured musicians were dashing all over town cramming in every available session. It was a good day's work for Sinatra, who cut three masterly love ballads - the intimate 'If I Forget You',

an attractive Alec Wilder song 'Where is the One?', and 'When is Sometime?', from Crosby's movie *A Connecticut Yankee in King Arthur's Court*, in which it was sung by Rhonda Fleming.

With the ban in force, Sinatra went into the studio on 16 March 1948 and dubbed vocals on to two stacked-up Stordahl backings, both Irving Berlin songs from *Easter Parade*. Surprisingly, the bouncy, lightweight 'A Fella with an Umbrella' scores over the more typical romance of 'It Only Happens When I Dance with You'.

The alternative to over-dubbing was to return to the a cappella sound that had enforcedly launched Sinatra's solo career during the previous Union ban. Nat 'King' Cole was clearly destined to win the 'Nature Boy' battle but Sinatra's was one of several competing versions, using the choir led by his radio-show arranger Jeff Alexander.

On 6 December he anticipated the end of the ban by recording a country strut, 'Sunflower' (clearly the melodic basis for 'Hello Dolly') with a non-Union and anonymous hillbilly group, who sported a fine steel guitar player.

In New York on 14 December Sinatra cut the Frank Loesser number 'Once in Love with Amy', backed only by pianist Henry Rowland. Bandleader Mitchell Ayres subsequently dubbed an arrangement around the track, presented here unadorned for the first time. Confusingly, on the following day and on the other side of America, Sinatra and Ayres recut the song. The rest of the day was devoted to small-combo jazz with The Phil Moore Four - the bluesy, late-night 'Why Can't You Believe' and a lightly swinging 'Bop! Goes My Heart'.

Stordahl and the full orchestra returned four days later for a half-hearted 'Comme Çi, Comme Ça'; the lush romance of Billy Eckstine vehicle 'No Orchids for My Lady'; and a version of 'The Three Bells' (initially by Piaf, and a 1959 number one for The Browns), here called 'While the Angelus was Ringing'.

With the studio ban over there was no call for another working Christmas, and Sinatra next recorded on 4 January 1949, again with The Phil Moore Four, producing a bouncy 'If You Stub Your Toe on the Moon' and the meditative Styne/Cahn song 'Kisses and Tears'.

A South Pacific session on 28 February resulted in a thoughtful, understated 'Some Enchanted Evening' and the nonsense of 'Bali Ha'i'. A trio of steel guitars and a vocal group ululating cod Hawaiian noises do not establish a life for this song outside the musical. Far more successful was the 3 March session, creating a lush, romantic feel for two strong ballads, 'The Right Girl for Me' and 'Night after Night', the latter distinguished by Herbie Haymer's tenor solo.

Long before Hank Ballard, let alone Chubby Checker - on 10 April 1949 in fact - Sinatra was persuaded to cut a somewhat polite R&B dance novelty. 'Wiggle like a snake, waddle like a duck' is just some of the advice dispensed during 'The Huckle-Buck'. It was a hit, though. The night's other offering, 'It Happens Every Spring', develops into a convincing love song.

Disc 10:

Let's Take An Old-Fashioned Walk/ (Just One Way To Say) I Love You/ It All Depends On You/ Bye Bye Baby/ Don't Cry Joe (Let Her Go, Let Her Go, Let Her Go)/ Every Man Should Marry/ If I Ever Love Again/ We're Just A Kiss Apart/ Every Man Should Marry/ The Wedding Of Lili Marlene/ That Lucky Old Sun (Just Rolls Around Heaven All Day)/ Mad About You/ (On The Island Of) Stromboli/ The Old Master Painter/ Why Remind Me/ Sorry/ Sunshine Cake/ (We've Got A) Sure Thing/ God's Country/ Sheila/ Chattanoogie Shoe Shine Boy/ Kisses And Tears/ When The Sun Goes Down/ American Beauty Rose

Sinatra's only record with Doris Day, his co-star in the 1955 movie *Young at Heart,* was cut on 6 May 1949 - the corny but acceptable novelty 'Let's Take an Old-Fashioned Walk'. The session was completed by the melancholy sentiments of Irving Berlin's 'I Love You'.

A successful day's work on 10 July, with arrangers George Siravo and Sy Oliver and a group of brass and rhythm players, produced the up-tempo jump tune 'It All Depends on You'; the mellow swing of 'Bye Bye Baby'; and a hit in the bluesy 'Don't Cry Joe'. Hugo Winterhalter temporarily took the baton from a holidaying Stordahl, and returned four days later to less effect for 'Every Man Should Marry' and 'If I Ever Love Again'.

On 21 July Morris Stoloff was in charge, and Sinatra kicked more life into 'Every Man...' at his second attempt. But 'We're Just a Kiss Apart' is ordinary and, though the elaborate string introduction to 'The Wedding of Lili Marlene' demands attention, this after-the-war song fails to develop.

Far more productive was a day with Jeff Alexander on 15 September, producing a hit with an energetic version of the Frankie Laine success 'That Lucky Old Sun'; a lush 'Mad About You', epitomising the strengths of the Sinatra/Stordahl partnership when working with first-rate romantic material

(Stordahl had left his arrangements behind when he went on vacation); and an Italianate adventure, 'Stromboli'.

Stordahl returned refreshed in the autumn, and for the next two sessions (30 October and 8 November) added the ex-Glenn Miller Modernaires vocal group to smaller-than-usual instrumentation. The jaunty 'The Old Master Painter' was a hit; 'Why Remind Me' is a big, effective ballad; while the romantic 'Sorry' and 'Sure Thing' have their moments. Variety was provided by a jaunty 'Sunshine Cake', with The Modernaires's Paula Kelly sharing the lead vocals.

On 12 January 1950 'God's Country' proved a somewhat dreary outing enlivened by a Ziggy Elman trumpet solo; and the romantic 'Sheila' bears a rare Sinatra co-composer credit. But the best-selling result of the day's work was a lively country-swing novelty, 'Chattanoogie Shoe Shine Boy'.

On 23 February The Voice met The Chest, and Sinatra duetted with Jane Russell on a lively version of 'Kisses and Tears', previously cut with Phil Moore but not released. The bluesy hill-billy of 'When the Sun Goes Down' was a more successful foray into hicksville than usual. By this time Mitch Miller had taken over from Sinatra's ally, Manny Sachs, as top music man at Columbia, and the first collaboration on 18 March showed promise - the strutting, confident 'American Beauty Rose' was a small hit.

Disc 11:

Peachtree Street/ Should I (Reveal)/ You Do Something To Me/ Lover/ When You're Smiling (The Whole World Smiles With You)/ It's Only A Paper Moon/ My Blue Heaven/ The Continental/ Goodnight Irene/ Dear Little Boy Of Mine/ Life Is So Peculiar/ Accidents Will Happen/ One Finger Melody/ Remember Me In Your Dreams/ If Only She'd Looked My Way/ London By Night/ Meet Me At The Copa/ Come Back To Sorrento (Torna A Surriento)/ April In Paris/ I Guess I'll Have To Dream The Rest/

Nevertheless (I'm In Love With You)/ Let It Snow! Let It Snow! Let It Snow!/ Take My Love/ I Am Loved/ You Don't Remind Me/ Love Means Love/ Cherry Pies Ought To Be You

Sinatra's name re-appeared as co-writer on 'Peachtree Street', a lively piece of nonsense cut on 8 April 1950 as a duet with the young Rosemary Clooney. Two further April sessions, with George Siravo as arranger and Mitch Miller in charge, were to produce material for the next Sinatra album, *Sing and Dance*. A frantic work schedule at this time meant that Sinatra occasionally encountered a singer's worst nightmare - he'd go for a note and his voice disappeared. And so the tracks were overdubbed, with the singer adding his contributions whenever he could.

Until this time the typical Sinatra vehicle was a lush love ballad cocooned in Stordahl's cascade of strings, but he was, of course, to prove a master finger-popper as well. These sessions were a giant step towards this new image. From the jumping 'Should I' to the dance novelty 'The Continental', the band boots along and Sinatra adds his totally confident swing phrasing. Ironic, then, that his career was about to take its dangerous down-turn, and that as an album these up-tempo gems were not a commercial success at the time.

Mitch Miller used just a trio of musicians and his own vocal group for a curious 'folk' session on 28 June. Admittedly 'Goodnight, Irene' was a competent production and a hit, just as it had been for polite folkies The Weavers, but if you want to hear the song properly stick to the bullnecked Leadbelly original. The sentimental 'Dear Little Boy of Mine' provided the B side.

Percy Faith conducted the band on 2 August but the sparky arrangement of 'Life is So Peculiar' sounds like Siravo, with Sinatra in relaxed, humorous vein. Stordahl was back in charge on 18 and 21 September, with mixed results. His wall of strings bolsters the melancholy ballad 'Accidents Will Happen', 'Remember Me in Your Dreams' is

FRANK WITH BOXING CHAMPIONS FRANK DEMPSEY (LEFT) AND JOE LOUIS.

pleasantly sentimental and 'If Only She'd Looked My Way' is a strong mid-tempo musing. 'London By Night', however, is something special - one can picture the singer strolling, happily alone, through an identifiable land-scape. The drawbacks to the session are a discordant 'Meet Me At The Copa' and above all (or, presumably, below all) 'One Finger Melody'. 'Yum di dah' sings The Voice. It was a big hit.

On 9 October Sinatra and Stordahl were on masterly form for a powerful 'April In Paris', one of the singer's great Columbia tracks. His vocals were never more tellingly controlled than in the ballad 'Nevertheless', further lifted by Billy Butterfield's trumpet. 'I Guess I'll Have to Dream The Rest', however, is routine (though it must be admitted that Sinatra's routine work is of rather a high standard!) while 'Come Back to Sorrento' is the sort of cod opera that seemingly he felt obliged to tackle occasionally. Sinatra is Sinatra, and Lanza is Lanza.

The Styne/Cahn 'Let It Snow...', a charming up-tempo exercise, made 5 November a successful day at the office, as was the session six days later. The deep-voiced smooch of 'Take My Love' is a steal from Brahms, while Cole Porter provided the Spanish-tinged 'I Am Loved' and a confident 'You Don't Remind Me'. On 11 December Rosemary Clooney returned, but 'Love Means Love' is forgettable and 'Cherry Pies Ought To Be You', while amusing in its by-play, was hardly a career landmark for either of them.

Disc 12:
Faithful/ You're The One/ There's Something Missing/ Hello, Young Lovers/ We Kiss In A Shadow/ I Whistle A Happy Tune/ I'm A Fool To Want You/ Love Me/ Mama Will Bark/ It's A Long Way (From Your House To My House)/ Castle Rock/ Farewell, Farewell To Love/ Deep Night/ A Good Man Is Hard To Find/ I Could Write A Book/ I Hear A Rhapsody/ Walking In The Sunshine/ My Girl/ Feet Of Clay/ Don't Ever Be Afraid To Go Home /Luna Rossa (Blushing Moon)/ The Birth Of The Blues/ Azure-Te (Paris Blues)/ Tennessee Newsboy (The Newsboy Blues)/ Bim Bam Baby/ Why Try To Change Me Now

The creative success of 16 January 1951, and a welcome if modest hit as well, was the lush ballad 'You're the One', with Stan Freeman contributing some telling piano. 'There's Something Missing' and 'Faithful', with Sinatra's voice seemingly and surprisingly uncertain, were forgettable. He next recorded three Rodgers and Hammerstein high-lights from The King and I, on 2 and 27 March. 'Hello, Young Lovers' and 'We Kiss in a Shadow' sound somewhat ponderous, and while the up-beat and innocent 'I Whistle a Happy Tune' is more successful, it remains a rather silly song.

Sinatra's re-visit to 'I'm a Fool to Want You' is in a different class, however. Stordahl pulls every romantic trick he can think of in the arrangement, and Sinatra is on top form. To me, nothing can equal Ketty Lester's smouldering revival of this song as the B-side to 'Love Letters', but Sinatra also knows what it means. His much-scrutinised relationship with Ava Gardner was in trouble at the time. Billy Eckstine scored more heavily with a competing version, but there was room in the charts for Sinatra as well. The day was completed by the slow melancholy of 'Love Me'.

'Mama Will Bark', a tongue-in-cheek duet with a statuesque but long-forgot-ten lady called Dagmar, assisted by a canine impressionist, marked a low

point of Sinatra's career on 10 May. Mitch Miller later defended this crap by pointing out that the punters weren't buying the good stuff as they once had, and so presumably anything was worth a try. It was a hit. A swinging 'It's a Long Way' was, by contrast, almost good.

On 19 July Sinatra was reunited with his old employer Harry James, who now had future bandleader Ray Conniff as trombonist and arranger, for a lively ses-sion. 'Castle Rock', a Johnny Hodges number, comes over as polite and early rock 'n' roll, as if Bill Haley had started as a jazzman instead of a hillbilly. It doesn't work, but it is engagingly over the top. 'Go get 'em, Harry, for old times' sake!' exhorts Sinatra. More suited to the pair are the smooth, muted 'Deep Night' and a return to 'Farewell, Farewell to Love'.

Dated 16 October, when it was mas-tered from the soundtrack of Sinatra's semi-autobiographical movie Meet Danny Wilson, is a strutting blues duet with Shelley Winters, 'A Good Man Is Hard To Find'. Given that Sinatra is no blues singer and Winters is no singer, period, it isn't too bad.

Sinatra's end-of-his-tether attitude to the insensitive and incompatible Mitch Miller didn't prevent his first session of 1952, on 7 January, being an excellent night's work. He was back in harness with Stordahl, and his smooth control throughout 'I Could Write A Book' is striking. The lush 'I Hear A Rhapsody' was another minor hit, but the highlight was a brassy, up-tempo strut through 'Walking In The Sunshine'.

On 6 February the romantic 'My Girl' and a bopping 'Don't Ever Be Afraid To Go Home' were successful, a verdict somewhat tempered by a dreadful piece of work called 'Feet Of Clay'. There was a long break until Sinatra's penultimate Columbia session, on 3 June, and the chosen repertoire has the stamp of Mitch Miller. The polite Latin beat of 'Luna Rossa', a nervous, jumpy version of 'Azure Te', the cowboy novelty 'Tennessee Newsboy' and the non-sense R&B of 'Bim Bam Baby' are all totally unmatched to Sinatra's

strengths. More successful was Heinie Beau's big brass arrangement for 'The Birth Of The Blues', with a lot of long-held notes for Sinatra, but as we have observed so many times, Sinatra could convey the blues but he was not a blues singer, which is what this song really needs.

With Percy Faith in charge but the spirit of Axel Stordahl undoubtedly present, Sinatra and Columbia Records ended their relationship with a session on 17 September. The mellow strengths of 'Why Try To Change Me Now' are surprising in the circumstances. Sinatra gave it one last shot and then, as he is alleged to have told his mother over the phone, 'fired Columbia'. With Mitch Miller immovably in charge of the label's A&R, it was the end of the road.

THE BEST OF THE COLUMBIA YEARS 1943-1952

Disc 1:
Close To You/ People Will Say We're In Love/ If You Are But A Dream/

Saturday Night (Is The Loneliest Night Of The Week)/ White Christmas/ I Fall In Love Too Easily/ Ol' Man River/ Stormy Weather/ Embraceable You/ (I Got A Woman Crazy For Me) She's Funny That Way/ My Melancholy Baby/ Where Or When/ All The Things You Are/ I Should Care/ Dream/ Put Your Dreams Away (For Another Day)/ Over The Rainbow/ If I Love You/ Someone To Watch Over Me/ You Go To My Head/ These Foolish Things (Remind Me Of You)/ The House I Live In/ Day By Day

Disc 2:

Nancy (With The Laughing Face)/ Full Moon And Empty Arms/ Oh, What It Seemed To Be/ (I Don't Stand) A Ghost Of A Chance/ Why Shouldn't I?/ Try A Little Tenderness/ Begin The Beguine/ They Say It's Wonderful/ That Old Black Magic/ How Deep Is The Ocean (How Blue Is The Sky)/ Home On The Range/ Five Minutes More/ The Things We Did Last Summer/ Among My Souvenirs/ September Song/ Blue Skies/ Guess

I'll Hang My Tears Out To Dry/ Lost In The Stars/ There's No Business Like Show Business/ Time After Time/ The Brooklyn Bridge/ Sweet Lorraine/ Always/ Mam'selle

Disc 3:

Stella By Starlight/ My Romance/ If I Had You/ One For My Baby (And One More For The Road)/ But Beautiful/ You're My Girl/ All Of Me/ Night And Day/ S'posin'/ The Night We Called It A Day/ The Song Is You/ What'll I Do?/ The Music Stopped/ Fools Rush In (Where Angels Fear To Tread)/ I've Got A Crush On You/ Body And Soul/ I'm Glad There Is You/ Autumn In New York/ Nature Boy/ Once In Love With Amy/ Some Enchanted Evening/ The Huckle-Buck/ Let's Take An Old-Fashioned Walk/ It All Depends On You

Disc 4:

Bye Bye Baby/ Don't Cry Joe (Let Her Go, Let Her Go, Let Her Go)/ That Lucky Old Sun (Just Rolls Around Heaven All Day)/ Chattanoogie Shoe

FRANK WITH DORIS DAY AND DIRECTOR GORDON DOUGLAS IN *YOUNG AT HEART*.

Shine Boy/ American Beauty Rose/ Should I (Reveal)/ You Do Something To Me/ Lover/ When You're Smiling (The Whole World Smiles With You)/ London By Night/ Meet Me At The Copa/ April In Paris/ I Guess I'll Have To Dream The Rest/ Nevertheless (I'm In Love With You)/ I Am Loved/ Hello, Young Lovers/ We Kiss In A Shadow/ I'm A Fool To Want You/ Love Me/ Deep Night/ I Could Write A Book/ I Hear A Rhapsody/ My Girl/ The Birth Of The Blues/ Azure-Te (Paris Blues)/ Why Try To Change Me Now

A sumptuous Digipak offering 97 tracks representing the Columbia decade on four CDs. The future of such collections must be in this Digipak format, effectively a hardback book the height of two CDs and the width of one, with the opportunity for extensive notes and artwork. No broken nails, no eyestrain, as with a conventional CD. Dealer resistance to the format has to be overcome, however, before they can become more commonplace. For all but the 'completist' fan who needs the comprehensive, chronological, track-by-track collection described above, this is an excellent and carefully-assembled summary of Sinatra's first ten years as a solo singer.

THE VOICE 1942-1952 (THE COLUMBIA YEARS)

One For My Baby/ I Should Care/ These Foolish Things/ I Guess I'll Have To Dream The Rest/ It Never Entered My Mind/ When Your Lover Has Gone/ Body And Soul/ That Old Feeling/ The Ghost Of A Chance/ There's No You/ Guess I'll Have To Hang My Tears Out To Dry/ Why Try To Change Me Now/ The Nearness Of You/ If I Had You/ Never The Less/ You Go To My Head/ My Melancholy Baby/ How Deep Is The Ocean/ Embraceable You/ She's Funny That Way/ For Every Man There's A Woman/ I Don't Know Why (I Just Do)/ Someone To Watch Over Me/ Love Me/ Saturday Night (Is The Loneliest Night Of The Week)/ Poinciana/ Try A Little Tenderness/ Autumn In New

York/ April In Paris/ Dream/ Nancy (With The Laughing Face)/ Put Your Dreams Away/ I'm Glad There Is You/ Day By Day/ Close To You/ I'm A Fool To Want You/ Should I/ The Birth Of The Blues/ Mean To Me/ It All Depends On You/ Deep Night/ Sweet Lorraine/ Castle Rock/ Why Can't You Behave/ My Blue Heaven/ S'posin'/ You Can Take My Word For It Baby/ Blue Skies/ The Continental/ It's The Same Old Dream/ Laura/ Stormy Weather/ I've Got A Crush On You/ The House I Live In/ All Through The Day/ I Couldn't Sleep A Wink Last Night/ Time After Time/ But Beautiful/ I Fall In Love Too Easily/ Brooklyn Bridge/ There's No Business Like Show Business/ The Song Is You/ September Song/ Oh What A Beautiful Morning/ They Say It's Wonderful/ Bess, Oh Where Is My Bess/ Where Or When/ I Could Write A Book/ Why Was I Born/ Lost In The Stars/ All The Things You Are/ Ol' Man River

Another four-CD collection, in this case offering 72 tracks.

16 MOST REQUESTED SONGS

All Or Nothing At All/ You'll Never Know/ Saturday Night (Is The Loneliest Night Of The Week)/ Dream (When You're Feeling Blue)/ Put Your Dreams Away (For Another Day)/ Day By Day/ Nancy (With The Laughing Face)/ Oh! What It Seemed To Be/ Soliloquy Parts 1 & 2/ Five Minutes More/ The Things We Did Last Summer/ The Coffee Song/ Time After Time/ Mam'selle/ Fools Rush In/ Birth Of The Blues

An 'official' variation on the 'best of' theme on Columbia Legacy.

SINATRA RARITIES - THE CBS YEARS

Why Shouldn't I?/ Two Hearts Are Better Than One/ The Girl That I Marry/ Could 'Ja?/ The Things We Did Last Summer/ Stella By Starlight/ So Far/ It Only Happens When I Dance With You/ When Is Sometime?/ Where Is The One/ Nature Boy/ Bop! Goes My

Heart/ It Happens Every Spring/ Accidents Will Happen/ London By Night/ Bim Bam Baby

A CBS release. All the titles are familiar, but maybe they qualify for rarity status because they have been less permutated than other material.

CHRISTMAS SONGS BY SINATRA

White Christmas/ Silent Night/ Adeste Fideles/ Jingle Bells/ Have Yourself A Merry Little Christmas/ Christmas Dreaming/ It Came Upon The Midnight Clear/ O Little Town Of Bethlehem/ Santa Claus Is Coming To Town/ Let It Snow! Let It Snow! Let It Snow!/ Medley/ Ave Maria/ Winter Wonderland/ The Lord's Prayer

A CBS compilation combines seasonal singles with radio material, sprinkled with unreleased and alternate takes.

SWING AND DANCE WITH FRANK SINATRA

Saturday Night (Is The Loneliest Night Of The Week)/ All Of Me/ I've Got A Crush On You/ The Hucklebuck/ It All Depends On You/ Bye Bye Baby/ All Of Me/ Should I?/ You Do Something To Me/ Lover/ When You're Smiling/ It's Only A Paper Moon/ My Blue Heaven/ The Continental/ Meet Me At The Copa/ Nevertheless/ There's Something Missing/ Farewell, Farewell To Love

The linking theme in this up-tempo Columbia set is that the arrangements are all by George Siravo. Although Axel Stordahl is the conductor more often than not, the master of the waterfall-of-strings approach usually deferred to Siravo when an injection of swing was required.

THE VOICE

I Don't Know Why/ Try A Little Tenderness/ The Ghost Of A Chance/ Paradise/ These Foolish Things/ Laura/ She's Funny That Way/ Fools Rush In/

Over The Rainbow/ That Old Black Magic/ Spring Is Here/ Lover

A 12-track, single CD collection from the Columbia years.

THE V-DISCS: THE COLUMBIA YEARS 1943-1952

V-Discs were wartime morale boosters (V in the Churchillian sense) made not for commercial release but for shipping to the armed forces - as such, they were among the first singles to be pressed in 'unbreakable' vinyl. This two-CD box contains 53 such titles by Sinatra, including six previously unknown ones, together with full discographical details. There is also a single CD on Bravura, *Sinatra: Portraits from the Past*, which collects some V-Discs and live broadcasts from the period.

THE RADIO YEARS (1939-55)

The young Sinatra's popularity was pinned as much to weekly radio broadcasts as to records, and there is a wealth of releases devoted to broadcast material. This, a six-CD, 125-track collection on Meteor, is the most comprehensive. It includes a couple of Harry James tracks and 18 with Tommy Dorsey as well as Sinatra the radio star, with 20 items from his series *To Be Perfectly Frank*.

There are many other rarity collections: *The House I Live In* (Vintage Jazz Classics) - mainly previously-unreleased broadcast tapes - *Live 1942-46* (Jazz Hour); *1949 Lite-Up Time Shows* (Jazz Band); *1946 Old Gold Shows* (Jazz Hour); *The Rarities 1950-51* (Voice) - in fact taken from Sinatra's early TV shows; *The Voice 1943-1947* (Decade); *Your Hit Parade 1944* (JR Records); *Your Hit Parade 1947* (JR Records); *Got the World On a String* (Starburst); *Harry James and his Orchestra: American Dances Broadcasts* (Jasmine); *Bandstand Memories 1938 to 1948* (Hindsight) - as with the previous title, this is a James record with some contributions by Sinatra; *Live*

Duets 1943-1957 (Voice), where the duettists include Dinah Shore, Bing Crosby and Nat 'King' Cole; a Pickwick collection on a similar theme, *Frank Sinatra and Friends, 1935-1939*; *The*

Beginning & Harry James (FS); *Perfectly Frank* (Bravura); *The Rarest Sinatra* (Decade); *Portraits from the Past* (Bravura); *Songs by Sinatra Vol 1* (International); *Tommy Dorsey & His*

Orchestra (Jazz Hour) - four Sinatra tracks; *Live at the Meadowbrook* (Jasmine) - as with the previous title, this is credited to Dorsey; *1942 War Bond Broadcast* (Jazz Hour) - ditto; *The Unheard Frank Sinatra Volumes 1 to 4* (Vintage Jazz Classics) - radio shows, including some rehearsals and run-throughs; and *Young Frank Sinatra* (Natasha).

Possibly the earliest solo-career recordings are on *The Complete Treasury Song Parade Shows*, featuring Sinatra with David Broekman and the Treasury Ensemble, which appear to date from the limbo between Dorsey and Columbia. *Frank Sinatra Sings the Songs of Sammy Cahn and Jules Styne* (Vintage Jazz Classics) celebrates the work of his most frequent writing collaborators, and is taken from Columbia-period radio broadcasts. Also sourced from radio, dating from the Forties and Fifties, is a handsome 20-tracker, *In Celebration*. *The Hollywood Golden Years: Greatest Original Soundtracks* (a title that suggests this is part of a series, perhaps) draws on *On the Town* and *Anchors Aweigh*; while a Bravura collection *The Soundtrack Sessions* ranges through *Meet Danny Wilson*, the 1954 animated feature version of *Finian's Rainbow*, *Carousel*, *The Man with the Golden Arm*, *The Joker is Wild* and *Advise and Consent*.

Although this wealth of material adds a vital chapter to the Sinatra story, and some - like the last-named - have a broader appeal, many of these records are only for the fan who needs everything. In the recording studio Sinatra was in charge - perhaps to a greater degree than any artist before him - while on radio it was the sponsor who ruled. It is noticeable, however, that where these collections are unofficial - either taking advantage of copyright laws or simply ignoring them (I have made no attempt to distinguish the two) - they are put together by enthusiasts rather than fly-by-nighters.

WITH FRANK SINATRA JNR AND DEAN MARTIN

The Capitol Years

In 1952, ten years after going solo, just a few short years after provoking levels of fan hysteria never before experienced, Sinatra's career was threatening to go into a tailspin. The hits were still coming, but they had become fewer and smaller, and he was being dropped by record company, booking agency, film studios, television and radio networks alike. There was no real boycott, of course, just a sudden and dramatic demonstration of the ups and downs of the pop music business. As Stan Britt has noted, if girls were screaming 'Frankie!' they were now jostling for Frankie Laine. Sinatra's long relationship with Columbia would formally end on 31 December.

But in the meantime he had come up with a career plan. After charming and crooning his way through some forgettable movies, including one or two real turkeys, he spotted a humdinger of a part - an actor's part, not an extension of his pop stardom. With vastly reduced bargaining power, but a conviction that the role of Angelo Maggio in the film version of James Jones's best-selling Pearl Harbor novel *From Here to Eternity* was made for him, and knowing that the movie was at casting stage, he set about landing the job. At least one actor, Eli Wallach, was already a front-runner, but Sinatra lobbied for a screen test. He even told Columbia Pictures boss Harry Cohn that he would work for $1000 a week - a fortune to most people at the time, a bargain-bin rate for a film star.

At last he got his test, and reached the final list of three along with Wallach and Harvey Lembeck. He lost out - the role went to Wallach. But the latter then withdrew after contractual disagreements and a tempting stage offer, and Sinatra was hired.

He worked on the movie during March 1953 and into April, learning hugely from that most subtle and intense of screen actors, Montgomery Clift. A

FRANK AND MIA FARROW.

year later, with the film winning five
Oscars from an almost unprecedented
13 nominations, including a Best
Supporting Actor award for Sinatra, his
extraordinary rehabilitation was complete.

But he was a singer above all, and so
this process could not have been complete without a record contract. Whilst
working on the movie he signed with
Capitol. And just as he had driven down

his price in an attempt to secure the film, so he had to accept a record deal that would have been unthinkable five years earlier. One of the most creatively fruitful relationships in record history, comparable with that of The Beatles with EMI house producer George Martin, began on a no advance basis, and Sinatra also had to stump up for the costs of musicians and arrangers. On April 2 1953, he recorded for Capitol for the first time.

After these sessions, during which he worked with both Nelson Riddle and Billy May, Sinatra spent the summer touring Europe, mainly in the UK. After a Las Vegas season in October, and a formal separation from Ava Gardner, Sinatra began work on his first Capitol album, *Songs for Young Lovers*, in November.

SONGS FOR YOUNG LOVERS

The Girl Next Door/They Can't Take That Away From Me/ Violets For Your Furs/Someone To Watch Over Me/My One And Only Love/Little Girl Blue/Like Someone In Love/A Foggy Day/It Worries Me/I Can Read Between The Lines/I Get A Kick Out Of You/My Funny Valentine

Sinatra may not have had the clout to arrive at Capitol on his own terms, but his timing could hardly have been better. The newly-developed vinyl, microgroove long-playing record could have been invented just for him, offering the prospect of 'an evening with Frank Sinatra'. From the very outset he exploited its potential to be more than a sequence of unrelated singles, though this was to remain a familiar album format until the present day.

Sinatra saw the long-player as a concert, a recital exploring a particular mood or theme - the 'concept' album. *Songs For Young Lovers* was the first - after limbering up with a few singles sessions for Capitol he was ready for the new format.

Arranger Nelson Riddle was assigned to the project, and his partnership with Sinatra was soon to prove as fruitful as Axel Stordahl's. And richer, if anything -

Riddle's music could swing as well as croon, whereas Stordahl's forte was the string-soaked romantic ballad, with any hint of an up-tempo mood usually being handed over to George Siravo. Having said that, it should be noted that the livelier items on *Songs For Young Lovers* were still conducted to Siravo charts, just like the old days.

Sinatra assembled a suite of 'young love' songs from such reliable sources as the Gershwins, Rodgers and Hart, Van Heusen and Burke, and Cole Porter. Eight tracks made up the original 10" album. On 5 November 1953 he cut the record's masterpieces, the Gershwins' 'A Foggy Day', during which 'the sun was shining, shining, shining, shining...', with Sinatra's voice fading from joy to reminiscence as he repeats the key word; and Rodgers and Hart's 'My Funny Valentine', a technical and emotional *tour de force*.

The day also produced a sprightly 'They Can't Take That Away From Me' and the atmospheric 'Violets For Your Furs', in which wintry Manhattan is cov-

ered in a 'fil-l-l-m-m' of ice. On the following day the lush 'Like Someone In Love', a joyous 'I Get A Kick Out Of You' and tender readings of 'Little Girl Blue' and 'The Girl Next Door' were added.

Was this really the Sinatra who had so recently, and so desperately, cavorted with Dagmar through 'Mama Will Bark'? Here, suddenly, was the mature performer in concert - what we had heard up until this point was a sequence of singles strung together, digitally remastered and put on to CD. Now he was consciously making 'art'.

When the 12" album became the norm, four further compatible titles were added, blending in unobtrusively and bolstering the theme. 'My One and Only Love' and 'I Can Read Between the Lines' had already been cut at the time of the album sessions - on 2 May 1953 - while 'It Worries Me' came from a session on 13 May 1954, and 'Someone to Watch Over me' - the outstanding 'bonus' track - on 23 September.

SWING EASY

Jeepers Creepers/ Taking A Chance On Love/ Wrap Your Troubles In Dreams/ Lean Baby/ I Love You/ I'm Gonna Sit Right Down And Write Myself A Letter/ Get Happy/ All Of Me/ How Could You Do A Thing Like That To Me/ Why Should I Cry Over You/ Sunday/ Just One Of Those Things

Sinatra's second Capitol album, (another eight-tracker later augmented, as *Songs for Young Lovers* had been, by four compatible tracks) was well titled. A gentle, confident swing dominates the mood, whether it be the bubbling 'Jeepers Creepers', the mellow 'Taking a Chance on Love', with Sinatra's swooping vocals cutting through the arrangement, or the finger-snapping kick of 'Wrap Your Troubles in Dreams'. The sessions, with Nelson Riddle in charge, took place on 7 and 19 April 1954.

The first added track fits in well, and it's a curiosity. 'Lean Baby' dates from Sinatra's first Capitol session on 2 April a year previously, when 'I'm Walking Behind You' was selected as the launch single (and put Sinatra back in the Top Ten). 'Lean Baby' is a polite but engaging R&B workout, co-written by Billy May, arranged by Heinie Beau, conducted by Axel Stordahl - though both remain scrupulously true to the May spirit.

'I Love You', another addition to the original format, is also in the May mould, though this time Riddle was responsible for the respectful pastiche. The song is somewhat routine, but the vocals and the booting arrangement lift it. Side one in vinyl format is completed by the jolly, walking groove of 'I'm Gonna Sit Right Down and Write Myself a Letter'.

Sinatra rides through a lively start to Side two, decorated with some intriguing rumbling brass figures. However, the strengths and depths of black gospel music are such that happy-clappy white contributions to the genre like 'Get Happy' always seem second best. A hip, defiant 'All of Me' more than compensates.

The next added track, 'How Could You Do a Thing Like That To Me', continues the mood but is somewhat out of time - it was recorded almost a year later than the 'real' album, on 7 March 1955. The full, brassy treatment of 'Why Should I Cry Over You', from 8 December 1953, makes sense as an addition since it was written by Ned Miller and Chester Conn, whose credits reappear on the jaunty 'Sunday'. Sinatra saves the best for last, though. The beautiful, arrogant control of Cole Porter's 'Just One of Those Things' produces the classic interpretation of a classic song.

SONGS FOR YOUNG LOVERS & SWING EASY

A 1992 double-CD combining the first two Capitol albums.

IN THE WEE SMALL HOURS

In The Wee Small Hours Of The Morning/ Glad To Be Unhappy/ I Get Along Without You Very Well/ Deep In A Dream/ I See Your Face Before Me/ Can't We Be Friends/ When Your Lover Has Gone/ What Is This Thing Called Love/ I'll Be Around/ Ill Wind/ It Never Entered My Mind/ I'll Never Be The Same/ This Love Of Mine/ Last Night When We Were Young/ Dancing On The Ceiling

This was conceived as Sinatra's first 12" LP, though in the UK it formed two 10" albums, and since being combined as one work it has appeared in slightly different configurations. Duke Ellington's 'Mood Indigo', which was indeed recorded during the sessions for this project, is absent from the most recent version. It is the first completely thematic expression of Sinatra's mature 'loner' persona, an extraordinary meditation on melancholy no doubt prompted by the crumbling of his marriage to Ava Gardner. And, as the singer approached 40, he had also achieved his first unalloyed masterpiece.

The central image in this ultimate mid-Fifties bedsitter companion is that of the singer in his lonely room, 'uneasy in his easy chair' as the lyric of 'It Never Entered My Mind' puts it. The title song

defines the parameters of the project, and at last we can see that this is Sinatra's own version of the blues, his own expression of soul. Nelson Riddle's arrangements chart the slow, quiet passing of the night hours, sometimes bolstered by ghostly strings, sometimes musing to a small-group setting. The singer will drift into sleep, or into a waking reverie, and see his lost love. She may be dancing on the ceiling, she may even encourage a fantasy of reunion, but then, just as he is 'Deep In A Dream', his cigarette burns down to his fingers and jolts him back to lonely reality.

The central song, perhaps, is Sinatra's aching interpretation of Hoagy Carmichael's 'I Get Along Without You Very Well', with all its reasons to contradict the defiance of the title. But there are rich variations on the theme - in 'I'll Be Around' the door is left open for a possible reconciliation, but in 'This Love Of Mine' the mood is closer to suicide: 'It's lonesome through the day, but oh, the night!' Of course, Sinatra was to return to the theme of 'Songs For Swinging Suicides' in the album *Only The Lonely*, but in three sessions during February 1955, and another early in March, he created a masterly blueprint.

SONGS FOR SWINGIN' LOVERS

Too Marvelous For Words/ Old Devil Moon/ Pennies From Heaven/ Love Is Here To Stay/ I've Got You Under My Skin/ I Thought About You/ We'll Be Together Again/ Makin' Whoopee/ Swingin' Down The Lane/ Anything Goes/ How About You/ You Make Me Feel So Young/ It Happened In Monterey/ You're Getting To Be A Habit With Me/ You Brought A New Kind Of Love To Me

Sinatra fans will of course differ on the choice of favourite album, and it may be that few devotees would actually plump for this, but it is surely the best-known nonetheless. Quite remarkably and probably uniquely, in the year that saw the tidal wave of rock'n'roll reach the shores of the UK, the album reached number 12 in the British singles charts! It would not be exaggerating to suggest that, in the case of many of the songs, they are as celebrated as they are simply because they were selected by Sinatra for this project. The contrast with *In the Wee Small Hours* could not be greater, and this in itself is a swaggering demonstration of versatility.

The album was recorded in January 1956, a month that saw Sinatra almost reach the top of the UK charts with the lightweight but charming 'Love and Marriage'. Nelson Riddle's arrangements are the perfect foil for an upbeat, confident and optimistic singer, whether they are bouncing off each other like sparring partners in Cole Porter's 'Anything Goes', or sharing a joke over the tongue-in-cheek 'Makin' Whoopee'. Another Porter standard, 'I've Got You Under My Skin', shows the perfect musical marriage between Sinatra and Riddle at its most confident, producing the definitive version of the song. And, once again, Sinatra has chosen a concept for the collection and then explored its every aspect: smoochy in 'You're Getting to be a Habit with Me', dramatic in 'Old Devil Moon' ('too hot to handle...'), jaunty in 'Swingin' Down the Lane'. An undisputed mood masterpiece, and in offering 15 tracks Sinatra was clearly revelling in the microgroove revolution.

CLOSE TO YOU

Close To You/ P.S. I Love You/ Love Locked Out/ Everything Happens To Me/ It's Easy To Remember/ Don't Like Goodbyes/ With Every Breath I Take/ Blame It On My Youth/ It Could Happen To You/ I've Had My Moments/ I Couldn't Sleep A Wink Last Night/ The End Of A Love Affair

A month after completing *Songs for Swingin' Lovers* Sinatra turned conductor for an instrumental album, *Tone Poems of Colour*, featuring arrangements by his collaborators Nelson Riddle and Billy May alongside such other luminaries as Elmer Bernstein and André Previn. Then in March 1956 he returned to the studio, with Riddle and the Hollywood String Quartet, Felix Slatkin, Paul Shure, Alvin Dinkin and Eleanor Slatkin, for another daring change of pace, style and mood. *Close To You* was completed at further sessions in April and October.

After the dance bands, Stordahl's string orchestras, Siravo's booting brass and Riddle's arrangements for medium-sized groups came the string quartet, though always bolstered by a rhythm section and coloured by solos

from flute, oboe, clarinet, French horn or trumpet. And the topic, conveyed in what the sleeve describes as 'his most intimate mikeside manner', is a rueful meditation on separation, love that cannot be accepted or achieved, unattainable love, and love threatened by 'that silly fight'.

This last danger is described in the collection's strongest song, Jimmy McHugh and Harold Adamson's melodic 'I Couldn't Sleep a Wink Last Night'. The overall tempo and mood is reminiscent of many Stordahl tracks, now in a chamber setting, but compared to the despair of *Wee Small Hours* the results are less striking. This may be, it must be admitted, because the songs dare to tackle more complex aspects of love.

A SWINGIN' AFFAIR

Night And Day/ I Wish I Were In Love Again/ I Got Plenty O' Nuttin'/ I Guess I'll Have To Change My Plans/ Nice Work If You Can Get It/ Stars Fell On Alabama/ No One Ever Tells You/ I Won't Dance/ The Lonesome Road/ At Long Last Love/ You'd Be So Nice To Come Home To/ I Got It Bad And That Ain't Good/ From This Moment On/ If I Had You/ Oh! Look At Me Now!

Sinatra and Riddle returned to the mood of *Songs for Swingin' Lovers* during four sessions in November 1956, resulting in another 15-track album (and a version of 'The Lady is a Tramp', which was not included on the LP). If anything, they have even more confidence this time round, with Riddle's up-tempo jazz arrangements at a new peak, most of them gradually building to a big, brassy finish.

Sinatra turned to some of the finest songwriters around - Cole Porter, Rodgers and Hart, the Gershwins, Jerome Kern, Oscar Hammerstein and Duke Ellington among them, with Porter responsible for four tracks. Though the atmosphere is always up-beat and optimistic, there is plenty of variation - a bold 'Night and Day'; a slinky, playful 'I Wish I Were In Love Again' (with its unforgettable but probably meaningless line 'When love congeals it soon reveals the faint aroma of performing seals'); a swaggering 'Oh! Look At Me Now!'; and a couple of bluesy interludes, tackled with more conviction than previously. Indeed, 'That Lonesome Road' threatens to expose all of Sinatra's blind spots together - gospel, folk and blues - but he handles it convincingly. One of the great Capitol albums.

WHERE ARE YOU?

Where Are You?/ The Night We Called It A Day/ I Cover The Waterfront/ Maybe You'll Be There/ Laura/ Lonely Town/ Autumn Leaves/ I'm A Fool To Want You/ I Think Of You/ Where Is The One/ There's No You/ Baby, Won't You Please Come Home

Another change of mood sees a return to wistful melancholy, together with two significant developments - this is the first Sinatra album to be arranged and conducted by, the next great collaborator Gordon Jenkins, and the first Sinatra album in stereo (though 'I Cover the Waterfront', with its shimmering strings evoking the scene, remains in mono). Jenkins wraps a rich texture around Sinatra's slow-tempo, carefully enunciated meditations. The arrangement for a return to the mysterious 'Laura' is a remarkable tonal ghost story, while another re-recording, 'I'm a Fool To Want You', is introduced by big, chiming chords. Two of the songs place Sinatra's mournful mood firmly in autumn, and whereas in 'In The Wee Small Hours...' he was alone in his room, he is now abroad in 'Lonely Town' singing the blues.

THE SINATRA CHRISTMAS ALBUM

Jingle Bells/ The Christmas Song/ Mistletoe And Holly/ I'll Be Home For Christmas/ The Christmas Waltz/ Have Yourself A Merry Little Christmas/ The First Noël/ Hark! The Herald Angels Sing/ O Little Town Of Bethlehem/ Adeste Fideles/ It Came Upon A Midnight Clear/ Silent Night/ White Christmas/ The Christmas Waltz (Alternate)

In July 1957 Sinatra and Gordon Jenkins cut a seasonal album released as A Jolly Christmas from Frank Sinatra, of which this 1991 collection is the current equivalent. As a CD it includes two tracks - the final two - recorded at the album session but not included on the original release. On vinyl it was more clearly divided into a 'modern' and a 'traditional' side.

COME FLY WITH ME

Come Fly With Me/ Around The World/ Isle Of Capri/ Moonlight In Vermont/ Autumn In New York/ On The Road To Mandalay/ Let's Get Away From It All/ April In Paris/ London By Night/ Brazil/ Blue Hawaii/ It's Nice To Go Trav'ling

Another landmark, the first credit to 'Frank Sinatra with Billy May and his Orchestra', distinguished this travelogue album recorded in October 1957. A mood of escapist fantasy is established with the title cut, and re-stated on what, in vinyl days, kicked off Side two, 'Let's Get Away from It All'. May's arrange-

ments vary the mood, from a stately 'Around the World' to the humour of 'Capri' and 'Mandalay'; the lush romance of 'April in Paris'; and the beautiful scenic evocations of 'Moonlight in Vermont', 'Autumn in New York' and 'London By Night', a masterly return to the song, when he reflects the 'magic abroad in the air'. The singer's unrivalled reading of 'It's Nice to Go Trav'ling' brings the journey full circle.

When the album was first released in the UK, in September 1958, 'Mandalay' was omitted as the Rudyard Kipling estate objected to Sinatra's jive-talk liberties with the original text of the poem.

ONLY THE LONELY

Only The Lonely/ Angel Eyes/ What's New/ It's A Lonesome Old Town/ Willow Weep For Me/ Good-Bye/ Blues In The Night/ Guess I'll Hang My Tears Out To Dry/ Ebb Tide/ Spring Is Here/ Gone With The Wind/ One For My Baby

During sessions in May and June 1958, following Wee Small Hours and Where

Are You? Sinatra took another long road into despair, perhaps the most daring of them all. The central image of the first collection, the lonely room, does at least offer some comfort and security, whereas now the singer is adrift seemingly without any hope. He even meets his lost love in 'What's New', having bid her 'Good-Bye'; and 'Ebb Tide' is twisted from its usual big-lunged expression into a wistful fantasy. This is one of four songs where natural imagery is used to mirror the singer's state of mind - willows weep for him, spring is here, but joylessly, and love has gone with the wind.

The singer has company, but cannot accept it. He even buys the whole room a drink in 'Angel Eyes', saying 'the drink and the laugh's on me,' before the stunning final line: ''Scuse me, while I disappear,' with Sinatra's voice, and Nelson Riddle's arrangement, withdrawing from the happiness they cannot share. One mark of Sinatra's command of mood is how he can invest standard lines of lost love with such poetic and dramatic depth - 'how I wish you'd come back to me,' 'love is gone,' 'I'll never forget you.'

This all leads us, of course, to one of Sinatra's most celebrated scenarios. It's a quarter to three, a blues piano doodles in the background among the upturned chairs, and Joe sets 'em up while the singer tells his tale of woe. A liner-note comment by Sammy Cahn and Jimmy Van Heusen, writer of the complex, mood-setting title song, suggests that *For Losers Only* was seriously considered as the name of the album. It is hard to imagine any record-company executive agreeing to such an off-putting idea, but it is a reminder that Sinatra, in spite of his tough-guy image, had no compunction in adopting this role.

COME DANCE WITH ME

Come Dance With Me/ Something's Gotta Give/ Just In Time/ Dancing In The Dark/ Too Close For Comfort/ I Could Have Danced All Night/ Saturday Night/ Day In - Day Out/ Cheek To Cheek/ Baubles, Bangles And Beads/ The Song Is You/ The Last Dance

True to the pattern he established during this great sequence of Capitol albums, of alternating melancholy with an up-beat, often humorous mood, Sinatra linked up once again with Billy May, who shared arranging duties with Heinie Beau, for another brassy, up-tempo, finger-snapping collection recorded in December 1958. And another pattern was to return to songs he had recorded earlier: 'Saturday Night' and 'The Song Is You' were first cut for Columbia. The sleeve of the album promised 'vocals that dance', and Sinatra lived up to the promise.

On vinyl, the next Sinatra album *Look To Your Heart* broke the sequence of thematic 'concept' projects by collecting together 12 songs originally recorded as singles, dating from 'Anytime, Anywhere' (May 1953). Three of the songs, including the title tune, come from his 1955 TV show *Our Town*. Nelson Riddle was in charge of all but one of the selections, the bluesy up-tempo 'I'm Gonna Live Till I Die', arranged by Dick Reynolds and con-

ducted by Ray Anthony. It was included in the re-release programme of 1984, which presented Sinatra's Capitol albums with impressive digital remastering.

NO ONE CARES

When No One Cares/ A Cottage For Sale/ Stormy Weather/ Where Do You Go?/ I Don't Stand A Ghost Of A Chance With You/ Here's That Rainy Day/ I Can't Get Started/ Why Try To Change Me Now?/ Just Friends/ I'll Never Smile Again/ None But The Lonely Heart/ The One I Love (Belongs To Somebody Else)

In March 1959, Sinatra was teamed once again with Gordon Jenkins, and the mood is similar to that of *Where Are You?* In other words, a return to melancholy, not as overwhelming and single-minded as *Wee Small Hours* and *Only The Lonely*, but often as powerful. The linking attitude is one of rueful resignation, exemplified by the aching 'I Don't Stand a Ghost of a Chance With You', and as well as the familiar use of weather metaphors for mood - storms and rain - there is the stunning conceit of Willard Robison and Larry Conley's 'A Cottage for Sale'. The singer stands outside the cottage as he stands outside a dead love affair, presumably a marriage, observing the overgrown garden, the blank windows, the overall feeling of neglect. Recent re-issues have included 'The One I Love...', a song recorded for the album but initially omitted, and its throbbing bass and jazz piano add variety to the programme.

NICE'N'EASY

Nice 'N' Easy/ That Old Feeling/ How Deep Is The Ocean/ I've Got A Crush On You/ You Go To My Head/ Fools Rush In/ Nevertheless/ She's Funny That Way/ Try A Little Tenderness/ Embraceable You/ Mam'selle/ Dream

Although the jaunty title track is slightly out of keeping with the arrangements on the rest of the album, it still sums up the feel of this collection. Sinatra was reunited again with Nelson Riddle, and

they cut these songs on the first three days of March 1960 with the exception of that first song, which dates from 12 April.

The mood, or theme, of the collection is less clear-cut than most of Sinatra's Capitol work. It is a romantic album, and at no point does Sinatra play either of his two most distinctive 1950s record characters, the loser and the hip, jazzy finger-snapper. Instead there is the confident, almost lazy, relaxation of a man at the top of his craft, smoochy on 'That Old Feeling', conveying awe at the hyperbolas of 'How Deep Is The Ocean', totally in command when returning to 'Try A Little Tenderness'. It does seem a slightly less rich experience, however, than the more straightforward demonstrations of either desolation or optimism that went before it.

SINATRA'S SWINGING SESSION

When You're Smiling/ Blue Moon/ S'posin'/ It All Depends On You/ It's Only A Paper Moon/ My Blue Heaven/ Should I/ September In The Rain/

Always/ I Can't Believe That You're In Love With Me/ I Concentrate On You/ You Do Something To Me

In his sleeve-note to the 1984 digitally-remastered vinyl re-issue of this collection, the late disc-jockey Alan Dell reveals why it gives comparatively short measure for a Sinatra album in terms of total running time. Apparently at the start of the first session - the tracks were cut on 22, 23 and 31 August 1960, completed on 1 September - the singer asked arranger Nelson Riddle to increase the tempo of most of the numbers.

Of course, any Sinatra/Riddle collaboration has rewards, and there are outstanding numbers here - a booting version of 'My Blue Heaven' that can stand alongside the warm, drawling million-seller by Fats Domino, and an exuberant 'You Do Something To Me' in particular - but a suspicion that was sown with *Nice 'n' Easy* is now growing. It seems that it is beginning to come a little too easily to Sinatra, and that in demonstrating his peerless way with a

song he has ceased to discover much for himself.

Significantly, only three of the songs are new to his repertoire - 'Blue Moon' (surprisingly overlooked until then), 'September in the Rain' and 'I Can't Believe That You're In Love with Me', the last-named another album highlight - and on several numbers the decision to increase the tempo makes the results seem somewhat hurried, unconsidered. Maybe if he had been envisaging these tempos from the outset, Riddle would have left more 'spaces' in the arrangements. This is an amiable and enjoyable outing, with singer, arranger and band melding slickly, but it is not one of the Capitol classics.

COME SWING WITH ME !

Day By Day/ Sentimental Journey/ Almost Like Being In Love/ Five Minutes More/ American Beauty Rose/ Yes Indeed!/ On The Sunny Side Of The Street/ Don't Take Your Love From Me/ That Old Black Magic/ Lover/ Paper Doll/ I've Heard That Song Before/ I

Love You/ Why Should I Cry Over You/ How Could You Do A Thing Like That To Me/ River Stay 'Way From My Door/ I Gotta Right To Sing The Blues

If the two previous Capitol albums did not seem to come up to the supreme standards Sinatra had been setting himself over the previous decade, all was not lost. By this time he had formed his own record company, Reprise, and was seeing out his obligations to Capitol. Maybe this prompted him into exuberance rather than time-serving, because the penultimate outing for his old label showed a distinct return to form.

His collaborator was Billy May, scoring and conducting the third and last of their *Come - With Me* albums. Again there were numerous returns to standards first tackled in the 1940s with Axel Stordahl at the helm, but now Sinatra showed new spirit. And May matched him with a bigger band than ever, with more brass and percussion, four French horns and a harp.

At the core of the programme was a long version of 'That Old Black Magic',

with Sinatra riding the lyric with all of his old command and curiosity. He still could not convince on a spiritual - 'Yes Indeed!' does not persuade us that he is a born-again gospel singer - but the reading of 'On the Sunny Side of the Street' is a delight, with the singer bouncing up against a playful arrangement, taking liberties with the lyrics to suit his mood. The last five tracks listed above are CD additions to the original vinyl release. The great Sinatra years may have passed, but the middle-aged crooner wasn't ready to give up completely.

POINT OF NO RETURN

When The World Was Young/ I'll Remember April/ September Song/ A Million Dreams Ago/ As Time Goes By/ There'll Never Be Another You/ Somewhere Along The Way/ It's A Blue World/ These Foolish Things/ As Time Goes By/ I'll Be Seeing You/ Memories Of You

By now Sinatra had already recorded three albums for his own company

Reprise, and his last Capitol long-player was a poignant one. There was certainly no sense of 'saving himself' for the new venture, and it is noticeable that the emotive title was not that of one of the songs, more a statement combining a reflection of the album's content with the stage that Sinatra's career had reached. He had chosen to strike out on his own once more, and contractually had reached the point of no return. For 35 years, at least - his career was to end back on the Capitol label.

He had last worked with his arranger from the Columbia days, Axel Stordahl, in 1954, but they were now reunited for an impressive farewell to the label that had established the mature Sinatra as the greatest interpreter of mainstream songwriting.

Although the word 'autumn' does not actually appear in any of the song titles, the abiding metaphor for this suite is of autumn as a time for looking back, ruefully and with melancholy, but also now with a new inner strength. Sinatra presents himself as the loner once again, but not as the desolate figure of Only the Lonely. He is a more European character, the romantic outsider, and the mood of the album is epitomised by his calm reading of 'I'll Be Seeing You'.

ALL THE WAY

All The Way/ High Hopes/ Talk To Me/ French Foreign Legion/ To Love And Be Loved/ River, Stay 'Way From My Door/ Witchcraft/ It's Over, It's Over, It's Over/ Ol' Macdonald/ This Was My Love/ All My Tomorrows/ Sleep Warm

As well as creating his series of concept albums for Capitol, Sinatra was of course also recording specifically for the singles market, and was a fixture in the Hot 100 throughout his time on the label. All 12 titles collected here were cut in partnership with Nelson Riddle, and all but two (the title track and 'Witchcraft') were in stereo.

Seven of these tracks made the charts: 'All the Way' (reaching number 15 in 1957, 3 in the UK), 'High Hopes' (30 in 1959, 6 in the UK), 'Talk to Me'

register today!

and experience the total betting service

bet by phone or online and pick up your winnings in cash – please ask us for details!

other ways to bet

(38 in 1959), 'French Foreign Legion' (61 in 1959), 'River, Stay 'Way from My Door' (82 in 1960, 18 in the UK), 'Witchcraft' (20 in 1958, 12 in the UK) and 'Ol' MacDonald' (25 in 1960, 11 in the UK).

AT THE MOVIES

From Here To Eternity/ Three Coins In The Fountain/ Young At Heart/ She's Funny That Way/ Just One Of Those Things/ Someone To Watch Over Me/ Not As A Stranger/ (Love Is) The Tender Trap/ Our Town/ Impatient Years/ Love And Marriage/ Look To Your Heart/ Johnny Concho Theme/ All The Way/ Chicago/ Monique - Song From 'Kings Go Forth'/ They Came To Cordura/ High Hopes/ All My Tomorrows

A third aspect of Sinatra's musical career was in recording songs for movie soundtracks, many of which also became chart singles. 'All The Way', the title track of the above singles album, was in fact one such example, since -

like another smash 'Chicago' - it came from *The Joker Is Wild*. Both songs were hits as a double-sided single in 1957. In the UK a similar compilation, Screen Sinatra, was released. The soundtrack albums to *High Society*, *Pal Joey* and *Can Can* have also been transferred to CD.

THE CAPITOL YEARS

I've Got The World On A String/ Lean Baby/ I Love You/ South Of The Border/ From Here To Eternity/ They Can't Take That Away From Me/ I Get A Kick Out Of You/ Young At Heart/ Three Coins In The Fountain/ All Of Me/ Taking A Chance On Love/ Someone To Watch Over Me/ What Is This Thing Called Love/ In The Wee Small Hours Of The Morning/ Learnin' The Blues/ Our Town/ Love And Marriage/ Love Is The Tender Trap/ Weep They Will/ I Thought About You/ You Make Me Feel So Young/ Memories Of You/ I've Got You Under My Skin/ Too Marvelous For Words/ Don't Like Goodbyes/ How Little It Matters How Little We Know/ You're Sensational/ Hey Jealous Lover/ Close To You/ Stars Fell On Alabama/ I Got Plenty Of Nuttin'/ I Wish I Were In Love Again/ The Lady Is A Tramp/ Night And Day/ Lonesome Road/ If I Had You/ Where Are You?/ I'm A Fool To Want You/ Witchcraft/ Something Wonderful Happens In Summer/ All The Way/ Chicago/ Let's Get Away From It All/ Autumn In New York/ Come Fly With Me/ Everybody Loves Somebody/ It's The Same Old Dream/ Put Your Dreams Away/ Here Goes/ Angel Eyes/ Guess I'll Hang My Tears Out To Dry/ Ebb Tide/ Only The Lonely/ One For My Baby/ To Love And Be Loved/ I Couldn't Care Less/ The Song Is You/ Just In Time/ Saturday Night (Is The Loneliest Night Of The Week)/ Come Dance With Me/ French Foreign Legion/ The One I Love (Belongs To Somebody Else)/ Here's That Rainy Day/ High Hopes/ When No One Cares/ I'll Never Smile Again/ I've Got A Crush On You/ Embraceable You/ Nice 'N' Easy/ I Can't Believe That You're In Love With Me/ On The Sunny

Side Of The Street/ I've Heard That Song Before/ Almost Like Being In Love/ I'll Be Seeing You/ I Gotta Right To Sing The Blues

A sumptuous, 75-track summary of Sinatra's Capitol career on three CDs. It is fine as a collection of singles, with each track taken as a complete entity, but of course the carefully-orchestrated mood concept of the 16-album series is lost - *Only the Lonely*, to take an obvious example, becomes a selection of tracks rather than a deliberately-considered suite exploring desolation. But it is undeniably pitched at one specific level of collector interest, and if it happens to be your level then this is a rich and varied selection of all the great tracks.

GREAT FILMS AND SHOWS
Night And Day/ I Wish I Were In Love Again/ I Got Plenty Of Nuttin'/ I Guess I'll Have To Change My Plans/ Nice Work If You Can Get It/ I Won't Dance/ You'd Be So Nice To Come Home To/ I Got It Bad (And That Ain't Good)/ From

This Moment On/ Blue Moon/ September In The Rain/ It's Only A Paper Moon/ You Do Something To Me/ Taking A Chance On Love/ Get Happy/ Just One Of Those Things/ I Love Paris/ Chicago/ High Hopes/ I Believe/ The Lady Is A Tramp/ Let's Do It/ C'est Magnifique/ Tender Trap/ Three Coins In The Fountain/ Young At Heart/ The Girl Next Door/ They Can't Take That Away From Me/ Someone To Watch Over Me/ Little Girl Blue/ Like Someone In Love/ Foggy Day/ I Get A Kick Out Of You/ My Funny Valentine/ Embraceable You/ That Old Feeling/ I've Got A Crush On You/ Dream/ September Song/ I'll See You Again/ As Time Goes By/ There'll Never Be Another You/ I'll Remember April/ Stormy Weather/ I Can't Get Started/ Around The World/ Something's Gotta Give/ Just In Time/ Dancing In The Dark/ Too Close For Comfort/ I Could Have Danced All Night/ Cheek To Cheek/ The Song Is You/ Baubles, Bangles And Beads/ Almost Like Being In Love/ Lover/ On The Sunny Side Of

The Street/ That Old Black Magic/ I've Heard That Song Before/ You Make Me Feel So Young/ Too Marvelous For Words/ It Happened In Monterey/ I've Got You Under My Skin/ How About You/ Pennies From Heaven/ You're Getting To Be A Habit With Me/ You Brought A New Kind Of Love To Me/ Love Is Here To Stay/ Old Devil Moon/ Makin' Whoopee/ Anything Goes/ What Is This Thing Called Love/ Glad To Be Unhappy/ I Get Along Without You Very Well/ Dancing On The Ceiling/ Can't We Be Friends/ All The Way/ To Love And Be Loved/ All My Tomorrows/ I Couldn't Sleep A Wink Last Night/ Spring Is Here/ One For My Baby/ Time After Time/ It's Alright With Me/ It's The Same Old Dream/ Johnny Concho Theme/ Wait Till You See Her/ Where Are You/ Lonely Town/ Where Or When/ I Concentrate On You/ Love And Marriage

Another even bigger catch-all collection on four CDs that cannot fail but include most of the great Sinatra tracks on Capitol, except of course those designed solely for one of the 'mood' albums.

20 CLASSIC TRACKS

Come Fly With Me/ Around The World/ French Foreign Legion/ Moonlight In Vermont/ Autumn In New York/ Let's Get Away From It All/ April In Paris/ London By Night/ It's Nice To Go Trav'lin'/ Come Dance With Me/ Something's Gotta Give/ Just In Time/ Dancing In The Dark/ Too Close For Comfort/ I Could Have Danced All Night/ Saturday Night (Is The Loneliest Night Of The Week)/ Cheek To Cheek/ Baubles, Bangles And Beads/ Day In, Day Out

Another formless but impressive collection, issued on the British label Music For Pleasure, which does include a notable sequence of Sinatra's great songs implying geographical location, mood and often season.

CAPITOL COLLECTORS SERIES: FRANK SINATRA

I'm Walking Behind You/ I've Got The World On A String/ From Here To Eternity/ South Of The Border/ Young At Heart/ Don't Worry 'Bout Me/ Three Coins In The Fountain/ Melody Of Love/ Learnin' The Blues/ Same Old Saturday Night/ Love And Marriage/ (Love Is) The Tender Trap/ (How Little It Matters) How Little We Know/ Hey! Jealous Lover/ Can I Steal A Little Love/ All The Way/ Chicago/ Witchcraft/ High Hopes/ Nice 'N' Easy

An interesting collection that only succumbs to the obvious towards the end.

THE FRANK SINATRA COLLECTION

Nice 'N' Easy/ Cheek To Cheek/ I'm Gonna Sit Right Down And Write Myself A Letter/ As Time Goes By/ Witchcraft/ I've Got You Under My Skin/ You Make Me Feel So Young/ I Can't Get Started/ I Get A Kick Out Of You/ Chicago/ Come Fly With Me/ The Lady Is A Tramp/ (Love Is) The Tender Trap/ My Funny Valentine/ Night And Day/ You'd Be So Nice To Come Home To/ Dancing In The Dark/ Let's Get Away From It All/ Nice Work If You Can Get It/ One For My Baby

As a 'best of' sprint this is probably as strong as you can get, concentrating on the familiar and rightly celebrated tracks.

FRANK SINATRA SINGS THE SELECT COLE PORTER

I've Got You Under My Skin/ I Concentrate On You/ What Is This Thing Called Love/ You Do Something To Me/ At Long Last Love/ Anything Goes/ Night And Day/ Just One Of Those Things/ I Get A Kick Out Of You/ You'd Be So Nice To Come Home To/ I Love Paris/ From This Moment On/ C'est Magnifique/ It's Alright With Me/ Mind If I Make Love To You/ You're Sensational

WITH SON FRANK JNR AND DAUGHTER TINA.

This would be a great anthology even if one didn't know that all the songs came from the same pen, undoubtedly the most suited to Sinatra of all those composers who didn't write specifically for him. There is also a CD collecting his Rodgers and Hammerstein material, and another 'select' compilation devoted to Johnny Mercer.

TWENTY GOLDEN GREATS

That Old Black Magic/ Love And Marriage/ Fools Rush In/ The Lady Is A Tramp/ Swingin' Down The Lane/ All The Way/ Witchcraft/ It Happened In Monterey/ You Make Me Feel So Young/ Nice 'N' Easy/ Come Fly With Me/ High Hopes/ Let's Do It/ I've Got You Under My Skin/ Chicago/ Three Coins In The Fountain/ It's Nice To Go Trav'lin'/ Young At Heart/ In The Wee Small Hours Of The Morning/ (Love Is) The Tender Trap

Yes, another album title you cannot disagree with, and these may be the Sinatra songs you want.

THIS IS FRANK SINATRA
1953-1957

I've Got The World On A String/ Three Coins In The Fountain/ Love And Marriage/ From Here To Eternity/ South Of The Border/ Rain (Falling From The Skies)/ The Gal That Got Away/ Young At Heart/ Learnin' The Blues/ My One And Only Love/ (Love Is) The Tender Trap/ Don't Worry 'Bout Me/ Look To Your Heart/ Anytime, Anywhere/ Not As A Stranger/ Our Town/ You, My Love/ Same Old Saturday Night/ Fairy Tale/ The Impatient Years/ I Could Have Told You/ When I Stop Loving You/ If I Had Three Wishes/ I'm Gonna Live Till I Die/ Hey! Jealous Lover/ Everybody Loves Somebody/ Something Wonderful Happens In Summer/ Half As Lovely/ You're Cheatin' Yourself (If You're Cheatin' On Me)/ You'll Always Be The One I Love/ You Forgot All The Words/ (How Little It Matters) How Little We Know/ Time After Time/ Crazy Love/ Johnny Concho Theme (Wait For Me)/ If You Are But A Dream/ So Long, My Love/ It's The

Same Old Dream/ I Believe/ Put Your Dreams Away (For Another Day)

Forty tracks on two CDs make up a well-programmed Music For Pleasure collection.

GOT THE WORLD ON A STRING: TWENTY CLASSIC TRACKS

I've Got The World On A String/ Them There Eyes/ If I Could Be With You (One Hour Tonight)/ Under A Blanket Of Blue/ Just You, Just Me/ Let's Fall In Love/ Hands Across The Table/ You Must Have Been A Beautiful Baby/ Someone To Watch Over Me/ I'll String Along With You/ Thou Swell/ You Took Advantage Of Me/ Where Or When/ This Can't Be Love/ Try A Little Tenderness/ Platinum Blues/ I'm Confessin'/ Sometimes I'm Happy/ My Funny Valentine/ That Old Black Magic

An unoffical CD on the Starburst label that juggles the familiar and the comparatively obscure.

LIVE BROADCAST PERFORMANCES 1953-1955

During these years Sinatra had a twice-weekly 15-minute show on NBC, *To Be Perfectly Frank*, during which he played current records and sang one song, with a small group including his longtime pianist Bill Miller. As we have noted before, Sinatra was a genius at exploiting the recording studio and its microphone almost as his instruments. On those occasions, of course, he was deliberately creating something for posterity. During his radio career, by contrast - and this is a good example - he was more relaxed, hardly expecting the material to resurface decades later.

FRANK SINATRA LIVE!
SEATTLE, WASHINGTON JUNE 9 1957
MONTE CARLO 14 JUNE 1958
A TOUR DE FORCE:
THE LEGENDARY CONCERT,
MELBOURNE, AUSTRALIA,
1959

Finally in this survey of the Capitol years, three 'unofficial' examples of Sinatra's concert performances. Ed O'Brien's note to the Seattle material says: 'The concert was recorded with the most advanced stereo technology of the time. The pristine sound of this performance is astonishing even by today's more exacting standards.' Sinatra was on a seven-date tour of the Pacific North-West at the time, with Nelson Riddle, Bill Miller and many of his regular Hollywood musicians.

The Monte Carlo set, put out by British Sinatraphile label JRR, has the additional curiosity value of an introduction by Noel Coward, who a couple of years earlier had recorded his clas-

sic - and career-reviving - live set at Las Vegas. The Australian concert, on Bravura, sees Sinatra performing with the Red Norvo Quintet.

The Reprise Years

Towards the end of Sinatra's years on Capitol, his ambition to own his own record label grew. One story has him driving past Capitol Tower in Hollywood and observing that he had helped to build it, and so it was now time to build one of his own. He was talking to an employee of the Verve label, Mo Ostin, and when Sinatra's dream became reality late in 1960 Ostin was appointed as executive vice-president, the man who actually controlled the company's day-to-day business.

Sinatra's first studio sessions for his own imprint were held on 19 and 20 December 1960, producing the tracks for the initial Reprise album *Ring-A-Ding-Ding!*, and on the following day he cut the first Reprise single, 'The Second Time Around'. On New Year's Day 1961 the label was officially launched.

In its first two years a number of Sinatra's friends were signed to Reprise, and the label took on a family/Rat Pack identity. Sammy Davis Jr (who came up with the first sizeable Reprise hit late in 1962 with 'What Kind of Fool Am I?'), Dean Martin, Jimmy Witherspoon, Nancy Sinatra, Bing Crosby, Nelson Riddle and Count Basie were early signings. The terms were unusual in that contracts were non-exclusive and that the artists rather than the company owned their own master tapes.

However, the company was fast going into debt, as a middle-of-the-road label in a market ever-more tuned to teenagers. Sinatra himself, however, had a commercial trump card - he was now an established box-office film star. Since Warner Brothers were keen to sign Sinatra the actor, a curious swap deal was hammered out to save the company. In 1963 Jack Warner bought two-thirds of Reprise, but gave Sinatra a one-third interest in the new company Warner-Reprise. He also got Sinatra's signature for a four-picture contract. At the time the record company was some $2 million in debt.

The story goes that, during the protracted and complex negotiations, Sinatra's finance lawyer Mickey Rudin mysteriously developed laryngitis, and that crucial negotiations with Warners' Steve Ross were conducted on restaurant paper napkins. As Ross explains in the book *Atlantic And The Godfathers Of Rock And Roll* (Fourth Estate Limited, 1993): "Neither one of us had a pad, and Mickey would write on a paper napkin. I didn't want him to have an advantage over me in time to think, so I would respond on a paper napkin. Those paper napkins are part of our files."

The first hit under the new deal was hardly a masterpiece - Lou Monte's long-forgotten 'Pepino, The Italian Mouse' - but Trini Lopez's 'If I Had a Hammer' improved the company's standing. In 1964 Reprise acquired the American rights to the successful British label Pye, home of Petula Clark (who gave Reprise their first gold disc with 'Downtown') and The Kinks.

Another 1965 smash was the song that Dean Martin pinched from Sinatra's back catalogue and made his own, 'Everybody Loves Somebody'.

1966 belonged to the Sinatra family - Nancy's 'These Boots are Made for Walking' and her father's number-one smash 'Strangers in the Night'. And a year later Reprise moved into the rock mainstream with Jimi Hendrix, Randy Newman and Joni Mitchell, followed by Neil Young, Ry Cooder and The Beach Boys (via a deal with the group's own Brother Records). Although the label was simply part of the vast Warners' empire it had by now established its own credentials, and was home to its founder until the early Nineties.

FAS: THE COMPLETE REPRISE STUDIO RECORDINGS

Disc 1:

Ring-A-Ding Ding!/ Let's Fall In Love/ In The Still Of The Night/ A Foggy Day/ Let's Face The Music And Dance/ You'd Be So Easy To Love/ A Fine

Romance/ The Coffee Song/ Be Careful, It's My Heart/ I've Got My Love To Keep Me Warm/ Zing! Went The Strings Of My Heart/ You And The Night And The Music/ When I Take My Sugar To Tea/ The Last Dance/ The Second Time Around/ Tina/ In The Blue Of The Evening/ I'll Be Seeing You/ I'm Getting Sentimental Over You/ Imagination/ Take Me/ Without A Song/ Polka Dots And Moonbeams/ Daybreak/ The One I Love Belongs To Somebody Else

Disc 2:

There Are Such Things/ It's Always You/ It Started All Over Again/ East Of The Sun (And West Of The Moon)/ The Curse Of An Aching Heart/ Love Walked In/ Please Don't Talk About Me When I'm Gone/ Have You Met Miss Jones?/ Don't Be That Way/ I Never Knew/ Falling In Love With Love/ It's A Wonderful World/ Don't Cry Joe/ You're Nobody 'Til Somebody Loves You/ Moonlight On The Ganges/ Granada/ As You Desire Me/ Stardust/

WITH DAUGHTER NANCY SINATRA

Yesterdays/ I Hadn't Anyone Till You/ It Might As Well Be Spring/ Prisoner Of Love/ That's All/ Don't Take Your Love From Me

Disc 3:
Misty/ Come Rain Or Come Shine/ Night And Day/ All Or Nothing At All/ Pocketful Of Miracles/ Name It And It's Yours/ The Song Is Ended/ All Alone/ Charmaine/ When I Lost You/ Remember/ Together/ The Girl Next Door/ Indiscreet/ What'll I Do?/ Oh, How I Miss You Tonight/ Are You Lonesome Tonight?/ Come Waltz With Me/ Everybody's Twistin'/ Nothing But The Best/ The Boys' Night Out

Disc 4:
I'm Beginning To See The Light/ I Get A Kick Out Of You/ Ain't She Sweet?/ I Love You/ They Can't Take That Away From Me/ Love Is Just Around The Corner/ At Long Last Love/ Serenade In Blue/ Goody Goody/ Don' Cha Go 'Way Mad/ Tangerine/ Pick Yourself Up/ If I Had You/ The Very Thought Of

You/ I'll Follow My Secret Heart/ A Garden In The Rain/ London By Night/ The Gypsy/ Roses Of Picardy/ A Nightingale Sang In Berkeley Square/ We'll Meet Again/ Now Is The Hour/ We'll Gather Lilacs In The Spring/ The Look Of Love/ I Left My Heart In San Francisco

Disc 5:
Nice Work If You Can Get It/ Please Be Kind/ I Won't Dance/ Learnin' The Blues/ I'm Gonna Sit Right Down And Write Myself A Letter/ I Only Have Eyes For You/ My Kind Of Girl/ Pennies From Heaven/ (Love Is) The Tender Trap/ Looking At The World Thru' Rose Colored Glasses/ Me And My Shadow/ Come Blow Your Horn/ Call Me Irresponsible/ Lost In The Stars/ My Heart Stood Still/ Ol' Man River/ This Nearly Was Mine/ You'll Never Walk Alone/ I Have Dreamed/ Bewitched/ California/ America The Beautiful

Disc 6:
Soliloquy/ You Brought A New Kind Of Love To Me/ In The Wee Small Hours

Of The Morning/ Nancy/ Young At Heart/ The Second Time Around/ All The Way/ Witchcraft/ How Little It Matters/ Put Your Dreams Away/ I've Got You Under My Skin/ Oh! What It Seemed To Be/ We Open In Venice/ Old Devil Moon/ When I'm Not Near The Girl I Love/ Guys And Dolls/ I've Never Been In Love Before/ So In Love (Reprise)/ Twin Soliloquies (I Wonder How It Feels)/ Some Enchanted Evening

Disc 7:

Luck Be A Lady/ Fugue For Tinhorns/ The Oldest Established Permanent Floating Crap Game In New York/ Here's To The Losers/ Love Isn't Just For The Young/ Have Yourself A Merry Little Christmas/ Talk To Me Baby/ Stay With Me (Main Theme From The Cardinal)/ Early American/ The House I Live In/ You're A Lucky Fellow Mr Smith/ The Way You Look Tonight/ Three Coins In The Fountain/ Swinging On A Star/ The Continental/ In The Cool, Cool, Cool Of The Evening/ It Might As Well Be Spring/ Secret Love/ Moon River/ Days Of Wine And Roses/ Love Is A Many Splendored Thing/ Let Us Break Bread Together

Disc 8:

I Can't Believe I'm Losing You/ My Kind Of Town/ I Like To Lead When I Dance/ Style/ Mister Booze/ Don't Be A Do-Badder/ The Best Is Yet To Come/ I Wanna Be Around/ I Believe In You/ Fly Me To The Moon (In Other Words)/ Hello, Dolly!/ The Good Life/I Wish You Love/ I Can't Stop Loving You/ More (Theme From Mondo Cane)/ Wives And Lovers/ An Old-Fashioned Christmas/ I Heard The Bells On Christmas Day/ The Little Drummer Boy/ Go Tell It On The Mountain/ We Wish You The Merriest/ Softly As I Leave You/ Then Suddenly Love/ Since Marie Has Left Paree/ Available

Disc 9:

Pass Me By/ Emily/ Dear Heart/ Somewhere In Your Heart/ Any Time At All/ Don't Wait Too Long/ September Song/ Last Night When We Were

WITH DEAN MARTIN (LEFT) AND SAMMY DAVIS JNR (RIGHT).

Young/ Hello, Young Lovers/ I See It Now/ When The Wind Was Green/ Once Upon A Time/ How Old Am I?/ It Was A Very Good Year/ The Man In The Looking Glass/ This Is All I Ask/ It Gets Lonely Early/ The September Of My Years/ Tell Her (You Love Her Each Day)/ When Somebody Loves You/ Forget Domani/ Everybody Has The Right To Be Wrong (At Least Once)/ I'll Only Miss Her When I Think Of Her/ Golden Moment

Disc 10:
Come Fly With Me/ I'll Never Smile Again/ Moment To Moment/ Love And Marriage/ Moon Song/ Moon Love/The Moon Got In My Eyes/ Moonlight Serenade/ Reaching For The Moon/ I Wished On The Moon/ Moonlight Becomes You/ Moonlight Mood/ Oh, You Crazy Moon/ The Moon Was Yellow (And The Night Was Young)/ Strangers In The Night/ My Baby Just Cares For Me/ Yes Sir, That's My Baby/ You're Driving Me Crazy!/ The Most Beautiful Girl In The World/ Summer Wind/ All Or Nothing At All/ Call Me/ On A Clear Day (You Can See For Ever)/ Downtown

Disc 11:
That's Life/ Give Her Love/ What Now My Love?/ Somewhere My Love/ Winchester Cathedral/ I Will Wait For You/ You're Gonna Hear From Me/ Sand And Sea/ The Impossible Dream/ Baubles, Bangles And Beads/ I Concentrate On You/ Dindi/ Change Partners/ Quiet Nights Of Quiet Stars (Corcovado)/ If You Never Come To Me/ The Girl From Ipanema/ Meditation/ Once I Loved/ How Insensitive/ Drinking Again/ Somethin' Stupid/ You Are There/ The World We Knew (Over And Over)/ Born Free/ This Is My Love

Disc 12:
This Is My Song/ Don't Sleep In The Subway/ Some Enchanted Evening/ This Town/ Younger Than Springtime/ All I Need Is The Girl/ Yellow Days/ Indian Summer/ Come Back To Me/ Poor Butterfly/ Sunny/ I Like The Sunrise/ Follow Me/ Cycles/ Whatever Happened To Christmas?/ The Twelve Days Of Christmas/ The Bells Of Christmas (Greensleeves)/ I Wouldn't Trade Christmas/ The Christmas Waltz

Disc 13:
Blue Lace/ Star!/ Gentle On My Mind/ By The Time I Get To Phoenix/ Little Green Apples/ Moody River/ Pretty Colors/ Rain In My Heart/ Wandering/ Both Sides Now/ My Way/ One Note

Samba/ Don't Ever Go Away/ Wave/ Bonita/ Someone To Light Up My Life/ Desafinado/ Drinking Water/ Song Of The Sabia/ This Happy Madness/ Triste

Disc 14:

All My Tomorrows/ Didn't We?/ A Day In The Life Of A Fool/ Yesterday/ If You Go Away/ Watch What Happens/ For Once In My Life/ Mrs Robinson/ Hallelujah I Love Her So/ I've Been To Town/ Empty Is/ The Single Man/ Lonesome Cities/ The Beautiful Strangers/ A Man Alone/ Love's Been Good To Me/ Out Beyond The Window/ Night/ Some Travelling Music/ From Promise To Promise/ A Man Alone (Reprise)/ In The Shadow Of The Moon/ I Forgot To Remember/ Goin' Out Of My Head

Disc 15:

I Would Be In Love (Anyway)/ The Train/ She Says/ Lady Day/ Watertown/ What's Now Is Now/ Goodbye/ What A Funny Girl (You Used To Be)/ Elizabeth/ Michael And Peter/

For A While/ Lady Day/ I Will Drink The Wine/ Bein' Green/ My Sweet Lady/ Sunrise In The Morning/ I'm Not Afraid/ Something/ Leaving On A Jet Plane/ Close To You/ Feelin' Kinda Sunday/ Life's A Trippy Thing/ The Game Is Over

Disc 16:

Bang Bang (My Baby Shot Me Down)/ You Will Be My Music/ Noah/ Nobody Wins/ The Hurt Doesn't Go Away/ Winners/ Let Me Try Again/ Walk Away/ Send In The Clowns/ There Used To Be A Ballpark/ You're So Right (For What's Wrong In My Life)/ Dream Away/ Bad Bad Leroy Brown/ I'm Gonna Make It All The Way/ Empty Tables/ If/ The Summer Knows/ Sweet Caroline/ You Turned My Life Around/ What Are You Doing The Rest Of My Life?/ Tie A Yellow Ribbon Round The Old Oak Tree/ Satisfy Me One More Time

Disc 17:

You Are The Sunshine Of My Life/ Just As Though You Were Here/ Everything Happens To Me/ Anytime (I'll Be

There)/ The Only Couple On The Floor/ I Believe I'm Gonna Love You/ Grass/ A Baby Just Like You/ Christmas Memories/ I Sing The Songs (I Write The Songs)/ Empty Tables/ Send In The Clowns/ The Best I Ever Had/ Stargazer/ Dry Your Eyes/ Like A Sad Song/ I Love My Wife/ Night And Day/ Evergreen/ Everybody Ought To Be In Love/ Nancy/ Emily/ Linda/ Sweet Lorraine

Disc 18:

Barbary/ I Had The Craziest Dream/ It Had To Be You/ You And Me (We Wanted It All)/ Macarthur Park/ Summer Me, Winter Me/ That's What God Looks Like To Me/ For The Good Times/ Love Me Tender/ Just The Way You Are/ Song Sung Blue/ Isn't She Lovely?/ My Shining Hour/ All Of You/ More Than You Know/ The Song Is You/ But Not For Me/ Street Of Dreams/ They All Laughed/ Let's Face The Music And Dance/ Theme From New York, New York/ Something

Disc 19:

What Time Does The Next Miracle Leave?/ World War None/ The Future/ The Future (Continued) (I've Been There)/ The Future (Conclusion) (Song Without Words)/ Finale: Before The Music Ends/ Bang Bang (My Baby Shot Me Down)/ Everything Happens To Me/ The Girl That Got Away /It Never Entered My Mind/Thanks For The Memory/ I Loved Her/ A Long Night/ South - To A Warmer Place/ Say Hello/ Good Thing Going

Disc 20:

Monday Morning Quarterback/ Hey Look, No Crying/ To Love A Child/ Searching/ Love Makes Us Whatever/ Here's To The Band/ All The Way Home/ It's Sunday/ L.A. Is My Lady/ Until The Real Thing Comes Along/ After You've Gone/ The Best Of Everything/ It's All Right With Me/ A Hundred Years From Today/ How Do You Keep The Music Playing?/ Teach Me Tonight/ If I Should Lose You/ Stormy Weather/ Mack The Knife/ The Girls I Never Kissed/ Only One To A Customer/ My Foolish Heart

IN *VON RYAN'S EXPRESS*.

This vast collection, entombed in a leather-bound, embossed coffin, presents every Sinatra studio recording for Reprise in chronological order, together with a hardback book of discographical information. What is lost, of course, is the sequence of original albums, though the compilers have taken care to avoid slicing thematic sessions in half by juggling the number of tracks on each CD. Also lost, or to be accurate relegated to small reproductions in the book, is the cover art of the original releases. The simplest solution has been adopted, and it is a massive and impressive project, but enthusiasts might feel that a better bet would have been to package together all the albums in chronological order, perhaps adding some out-take and rarity CDs along the way.

RING-A-DING DING!

Ring-A-Ding Ding!/ Let's Fall In Love/ In The Still Of The Night/ A Foggy Day/ Let's Face The Music And Dance/ You'd Be So Easy To Love/ A Fine Romance/ The Coffee Song/ Be Careful, It's My Heart/ I've Got My Love To Keep Me Warm/ You And The Night And The Music/ When I Take My Sugar To Tea/ Have You Met Miss Jones?/ Zing Went The Strings Of My Heart

In anticipation of the official launch of his record label, Sinatra and arranger Johnny Mandel went into the studio on 19 and 20 December 1960 to cut his début on Reprise. The last track listed did not appear on the original vinyl release, but completes the CD version. Although Sinatra could presumably not have used his most consistent arranger, Nelson Riddle, even if he had wanted to - Riddle remained a Capitol signing - the choice of Mandel is surely significant. His reputation was established in the 50s as a jazz composer, and the result is that Sinatra deliberately came up with a sharp, jazzy, swinging album as his first homegrown outing. The cover-art portrait, with his familiar hat at an even more rakish angle than usual, his fingers flicking his bow-tie, reflected the hip, cocky mood of this excellent set.

MORE RING-A-DING DING (LABEL UNKNOWN)

This unofficial release offers alternate takes and 'actual recording studio chatter' from the sessions for Sinatra's first Reprise album.

SINATRA SWINGS

The Curse Of An Aching Heart/ Love Walked In/ Please Don't Talk About Me When I'm Gone/ Have You Met Miss Jones?/ Don't Be That Way/ I Never Knew/ Falling In Love With Love/ It's A Wonderful World/ Don't Cry Joe/ You're Nobody Till Somebody Loves You/ Moonlight On The Ganges/ Granada

The jazz feel continued in a reunion with the most jazz-oriented of Sinatra's pre-Mandel arrangers, Billy May, cut in three days in late May 1961. A session imme-

diately prior to this, also with May providing the charts, failed to produce any released masters. This album justifies its title, particularly in a snappy rendition of 'You're Nobody...', without achieving the consistency of the Mandel set.

I REMEMBER TOMMY

I'll Be Seeing You/ I'm Getting Sentimental Over You/ Imagination/ Take Me/ Without A Song/ Polka Dots And Moonbeams/ Daybreak/ The One I Love Belongs To Somebody Else/ There Are Such Things/ It's Always You/ It Started All Over Again/ East Of The Sun

The third Reprise disc (in fact recorded a fortnight prior to *Sinatra Swings*) introduces a third arranger, ex-Dorsey man Sy Oliver, in this tribute to his and Sinatra's former employer. But both men have re-thought the old material, adding an extra dimension to the project. 'Without A Song' was previously done almost as cod operetta, but is a real finger-snapper on this version. This became Sinatra's third 1961 release.

SINATRA & STRINGS

As You Desire Me/ Stardust/ Yesterday/ I Hadn't Anyone Till You/ It Might As Well Be Spring/ Prisoner Of Love/ That's All/ Don't Take Your Love From Me/ Misty/ Come Rain Or Come Shine/ Night And Day/ All Or Nothing At All

The fourth Reprise album brought in a fourth arranger in Don Costa, whose contribution echoes Axel Stordahl's in cushioning a top-class collection of largely-familiar ballads in a lush, romantic setting. Although the tone of the songs in general recalls much of Sinatra's work on Columbia, there is now a new depth, a greater maturity, and perhaps a little more burr of experience in his voice. In the middle ground of Sinatra's albums, pitched between the hip swingers and the Great Depression, this February 1962 release stands as one of his most consistently accomplished.

SINATRA AND SWINGIN' BRASS

I'm Beginning To See The Light/ I Get A Kick Out Of You/ Ain't She Sweet/ I Love You/ They Can't Take That Away From Me/ Love Is Just Around The Corner/ At Long Last Love/ Serenade In Blue/ Goody, Goody/ Don'cha Go 'Way Mad/ Tangerine/ Pick Yourself Up

The revolving door through which arrangers arrived at and left Sinatra sessions continued to operate, and it was now Neal Hefti's turn. His previous credentials, including a decade with Count Basie and Forties stints with such names as Woody Herman, Charlie Ventura and Harry James, confirmed that this release, recorded in two April 1962 sessions, was a return to the swinging jazz mood of the first Reprise set. It also marked a contrast with its immediate predecessor - from cascading strings to none at all - and was a tight and joyful album.

ALL ALONE

The Song Is Ended/ All Alone/ Charmaine/ When I Lost You/ Remember/ Together/ The Girl Next Door/ Indiscreet/ What'll I Do?/ Oh How I Miss You Tonight

The sixth Reprise album (and therefore the sixth arranger - a reunion with Gordon Jenkins) was in fact cut before its predecessor, in January 1962, for October release. This could have suggested a certain queasiness at the overall quality, though it appeared nonetheless. Jenkins had proved a great collaborator in the past, of course, and there are one or two bull's-eyes, notably Irving Berlin's 'When I Lost You', but this is not a consistently striking album. Another track recorded for inclusion but omitted was intended to give the project its title - 'Come Waltz with Me' - and maybe this is the key to any disappointment one might feel. An album of waltzes, particularly when it includes such schmaltz as 'Charmaine', would perhaps need the entire family Strauss to maintain interest.

GREAT SONGS FROM GREAT BRITAIN

If I Had You/ The Very Thought Of You/ I'll Follow My Secret Heart/ A Garden In The Rain/ London By Night/ The Gypsy/ Roses Of Picardy/ A Nightingale Sang In Berkeley Square/ We'll Meet Again/ Now Is The Hour/ We'll Gather Lilacs

Summer 1962 was devoted to a Sinatra world tour, largely in the UK, and in June he and arranger Robert Farnon took over a London studio to cut a selection of British songs in front of an invited audience. Its release coincided with that of *All Alone*, perhaps compounding one's suspicion that the company were not entirely happy with either. 'London By Night' proves once again to be a great song indeed, but such wartime morale-boosting tear-jerkers as 'We'll Meet Again' belong exclusively to Dame Vera Lynn - and that bloody nightingale is still singing.

LONDON ROYAL FESTIVAL HALL 1 JUNE 1962 (JRR)

Goody Goody/ Imagination/ At Long Last Love/ Moonlight In Vermont/ Without A Song/ Day In, Day Out/ The Moon Was Yellow/ I've Got You Under My Skin/ I Get A Kick Out Of You/ The Second Time Around/ Too Marvelous For Words/ My Funny Valentine/ In The Still Of The Night/ My Blue Heaven/ April In Paris/ You're Nobody Till Somebody Loves You/ They Can't Take That Away From Me/ All The Way/ Chicago/ Night And Day/ Autumn Leaves/ I Could Have Danced All Night/ One For My Baby/ A Foggy Day/ Ol' Man River/ You Make Me Feel So Young/ Nancy/ Come Fly With Me/ Young At Heart/ In The Still Of The Night/ At Long Last Love/ All The Way/ I Love Paris/ The Lady Is A Tramp/ I Could Have Danced All Night/ In The Still Of The Night/ Without A Song

With the star picking up the expenses tab, much of 1962 was devoted to a world tour raising money for children's charities, with a six-piece group including regular pianist Bill Miller and guitarist Al Viola.

THE PARIS CONCERT 1962 (ENCORE)

No track details.

'Available for the first time (1992): Frank's rousing première performance in France.' This was another stop on his tour on behalf of children's charities.

SINATRA-BASIE

Nice Work If You Can Get It/ Please Be Kind/ I Won't Dance/ Learnin' The Blues/ I'm Gonna Sit Right Down And Write Myself A Letter/ I Only Have Eyes For You/ My Kind Of Girl/ Pennies From Heaven/ (Love Is) The Tender Trap/ Looking At The World Through Rose Colored Glasses

For the first time in the Reprise series an arranger was re-hired - Neal Hefti was called upon to write the charts for this collaboration between two of the greatest names in jazz. Sessions were held in October 1962 for release the following January: 'An historic musical first', proclaimed the album sleeve. And the results were predictably impressive, if often slightly stilted - it wasn't until their third album together, the live Sinatra at the Sands, that this mutual admiration society could gel together, swing together, well enough to live up to the combined weight of their billing.

THE CONCERT SINATRA

I Have Dreamed/ My Heart Stood Still/ Lost In The Stars/ Bewitched/ This Nearly Was Mine/ You'll Never Walk Alone/ Ol' Man River/ Soliloquy

Nelson Riddle was now available to work with Sinatra once more (their actual reunion had been a January 1963 session that produced the single 'Come Blow Your Horn'), and in February they went into the Hollywood studio with a vast 60-piece orchestra. Although the first two tracks proved impressive addi-

tions to Sinatra's repertoire, it was becoming apparent at this time that he still felt more comfortable looking backwards into his past catalogue when selecting songs - something that was of course to change quite dramatically, and with varying results, as he grappled with the age of rock. But these are not tired repeats - the *Carousel* blockbuster 'Soliloquy', for example, gains even more force than previously.

SINATRA'S SINATRA

I've Got You Under My Skin/ In The Wee Small Hours Of The Morning/ Second Time Around/ Nancy/ Witchcraft/ Young At Heart/ All The Way/ How Little We Know/ Pocketful Of Miracles/ Oh What It Seemed To Be/ Call Me Irresponsible/ Put Your Dreams Away

Clearly neither Sinatra nor Riddle had any doubts about the success of their reunion, since within two months of cutting *The Concert Sinatra* they reconvened in the studio. But this time the

danger inherent but overcome in the previous outing, cannot be ignored: all the material was drawn from Sinatra's back pages, and on this occasion little new was discovered. However, there's no such thing as a bad Sinatra/Riddle album, even when they seem to be treading water.

The rest of 1963 was marked by a series of singles dates, many of them duetting with such as Dean Martin, Sammy Davis Jr, Keely Smith, Rosemary Clooney and Bing Crosby. In August the merger with Warner Brothers put a million-dollar cheque in Sinatra's wallet, but in the same month the premature death, at the age of 50, of Sinatra's earliest arranging partner Axel Stordahl was announced. Two non-musical events should be noted here: on 22 November President Kennedy was assassinated, and on 8 December Sinatra's son Frank Jr was kidnapped, held to ransom, and subsequently rescued.

DAYS OF WINE AND ROSES

Days Of Wine And Roses/ Moon River/ The Way You Look Tonight/ Three Coins In The Fountain/ In The Cool, Cool, Cool Of The Evening/ Secret Love/ Swinging On A Star/ It Might As Well Be Spring/ The Continental/ Love Is A Many Splendored Thing/ All The Way

This further Sinatra/Riddle collaboration, fully, but somewhat cumbersomely entitled *Days of Wine and Roses, Moon River and Other Academy Award Winners*, was cut in January 1964 and showed that the pioneer of the theme album was still alive to its possibilities. The overall quality was far more satisfying than that of the previous release,

though Sinatra sounds a trifle awkward when confessing to a 'Secret Love'.

IT MIGHT AS WELL BE SWING

Fly Me To The Moon/ I Wish You Love/ I Believe In You/ More/ I Can't Stop Loving You/ Hello, Dolly!/ I Wanna Be Around/ The Best Is Yet To Come/ The Good Life/ Wives And Lovers

The second Sinatra-Basie album, cut in June 1964 with Quincy Jones providing the charts, surprisingly showed that such a stunning line-up could still not guarantee great grooves, although 'Fly Me to the Moon' gave a tantalising hint that they might have cracked it.

SOFTLY AS I LEAVE YOU

Emily/ Here's To The Losers/ Dear Heart/ Come Blow Your Horn/ Love Isn't Just For The Young/ I Can't Believe I'm Losing You/ Pass Me By/ Softly As I Leave You/ Available/ Somewhere In Your Heart/ Tell Her You Love Her Each Day/ When Somebody Loves You

A bit of a mish-mash recorded at various sessions in the second half of 1964 with three arrangers - Ernie Freeman, Nelson Riddle and Billy May - and producer Jimmy Bowen.

SEPTEMBER OF MY YEARS

The September Of My Years/ How Old Am I?/ Don't Wait Too Long/ It Gets Lonely Early/ This Is All I Ask/ Last Night When We Were Young/ The Man In The Looking Glass/ It Was A Very Good Year/ When The Wind Was Green/ Hello, Young Lovers/ I See It Now/ Once Upon A Time/ September Song

If the Chairman of the Board was to assess his first few years on his own label at this point, he could no doubt feel satisfied in reporting to the shareholders. The albums had dutifully charted and, in the face of British beat groups and Californian surfers, his singles had, by and large, followed each other into the Hot Hundred - even if none of them had progressed to the heights.

In spite of moments of magic, however, what was missing as far as the enthusiast was concerned was that consistent sense of artistry, of an *auteur* at work, that Sinatra had established during the mid-Fifties with his great series of thematic albums. He had barely come to terms with up-to-date songwriting, and when he looked backwards he often added nothing to previous readings of familiar songs.

All that changed, however briefly, with this album, the first Reprise masterpiece. It was recorded on three April nights in Hollywood, completed a month later, and Gordon Jenkins was back with the charts and the baton. Sinatra's 50th birthday was approaching, and though this landmark is more than halfway through our Biblical span, it is a symbolic moment, the time when - however reluctantly - we recognise that 'middle age' has arrived. Sinatra took this as a cue for a great concept album, a suite of reflective, mature songs. The voice was bruised but strong, searching for a rueful, melancholy or simply peaceful path through the lyrics, and it had never been better served by Jenkins' arrangements.

If a late-night disc-jockey wished to establish a particular mood on his programme, the mood explored by Sinatra throughout this collection, he could drop the needle at the start of any one of the numbers and the job would be done. This is where 'greatest hits' collections, however useful, break down: they destroy the mood. The only thing that would prevent this album sitting comfortably in the Capitol sequence is that he needed to be in his fiftieth year to tackle it.

MY KIND OF BROADWAY

Lost In The Stars/ Everybody Has The Right To Be Wrong/ I'll Only Miss Her When I Think Of Her/ Golden Moment/ Hello, Dolly!/ Have You Met Miss Jones?/ Yesterdays/ They Can't Take That Away From Me/ Nice Work If You Can Get It/ Without A Song/ Luck Be A Lady

Recorded at several sessions in the second half of 1965, with three arrangers in Torrie Zito, Billy May and Nelson Riddle, there are few surprises in this selection of Broadway successes, a sense of marking time while recycling largely familiar material.

A MAN AND HIS MUSIC

An ambitious departure from the normal run of Sinatra albums, this two-CD set is in effect a musical autobiography narrated by Sinatra, studded with renditions of 31 of his most familiar songs, and assembled by his usual producer of this period, Sonny Burke. Nelson Riddle, Billy May, Gordon Jenkins, Johnny Mandel, Sy Oliver, Don Costa and Ernie Freeman are among the arrangers.

STRANGERS IN THE NIGHT

Strangers In The Night/ Summer Wind/ All Or Nothing At All/ Call Me/ You're Driving Me Crazy/ On A Clear Day/ My Baby Just Cares For Me/ Downtown/ Yes Sir, That's My Baby/ The Most Beautiful Girl In The World

The title track, which was to put Sinatra back on top of the singles charts after many years, began life as a Bert Kaempfert instrumental, and Sinatra cut his lyric version on 11 April 1966, borrowing time from a Dean Martin session. This hurried piece of work, arranged by Ernie Freeman, was allegedly produced because other artists were planning to cut the song, but A&R man Jimmy Bowen felt it was tailor-made for Sinatra. Nelson Riddle was in charge for the remainder of the album material.

The album followed the title track up the charts, and 'Strangers...' took two Grammy awards for Best Solo Vocal and Record of the Year. As Nancy Sinatra reveals in her book *Frank Sinatra My Father,* he didn't care for the song, and with hindsight maybe we can hear a certain lack of involvement. But, after all these years, it is in fact a little difficult to hear anything in the number, such a monster did it become. Do-be-do-be-do. In America Sinatra kicked The Beatles' 'Paperback Writer' off the top of the charts, only to be replaced by the punkish 'Hanky Panky' by Tommy James and The Shondells. In the UK he followed The Rolling Stones' 'Paint It Black' and preceded The Beatles. As the rock era dawned, it was a remarkable achievement, but the album bearing its name showed some signs of being a stitched-together job.

MOONLIGHT SINATRA

Moonlight Becomes You/ Moon Song/ Moonlight Serenade/ Reaching For The Moon/ I Wished On The Moon/ Oh, You Crazy Moon/ The Moon Got In My Eyes/ Moonlight Mood/ Moon Love/ The Moon Was Yellow

Cut back in November 1965 with producer Sonny Burke and arranger Nelson Riddle, but presumably delayed because of the 'Strangers in the Night' kerfuffle, this showed a return to the 'concept' album with a sequence of ballads with 'Moon' in the title. It did not prove to be one of Sinatra's most successful themes.

SUPERB SINATRA (ENCORE)

No track details.

A 1990 issue billed as 'a newly discovered set of nightclub performances from the early 60s'.

GOLDEN AGE: A MAN AND HIS MUSIC (FREMUS)

I've Got You Under My Skin/ Without A Song/ Don't Worry 'Bout Me /I Get A Kick Out Of You/ Nancy/ My Kind Of Town/ Medley/ Come Fly With Me/ The Lady Is A Tramp/ I've Got The World On A String/ Witchcraft/ You Make Me Feel So Young/ Angel Eyes/ Come Fly With Me/ Night And Day/ Witchcraft/ A Foggy Day/ The Lady Is A Tramp/ Imagination/ Chicago/ My Blue Heaven/ I Love Paris/ I've Got You Under My Skin/ My Funny Valentine/ Moonlight In Vermont

The tracks down to 'Angel Eyes' are from a live recording dated 24

November 1965, and the remainder are billed as 'bonus tracks' from May 1962.

SINATRA AT THE SANDS

Come Fly With Me/ I've Got A Crush On You/ I've Got You Under My Skin/ The Shadow Of Your Smile/ Street Of Dreams/ One For My Baby/ Fly Me To The Moon/ One O'clock Jump/ You Make Me Feel So Young/ All Of Me/ September Of My Years/ Get Me To The Church On Time/ It Was A Very Good Year/ Don't Worry 'Bout Me/ Makin' Whoopee/ Where Or When/ Angel Eyes/ My Kind Of Town

On this double-set the Sinatra-Basie partnership clicked at the third attempt, with what was surprisingly the singer's first 'live' album. In January 1966 the duo were booked for a season at the Sands Hotel in Las Vegas, with Quincy Jones once more providing the charts. The shows were taped and the album was spliced together from peak performances. Sinatra clearly took the dates seriously since he flew the Basie band

WITH TOM JONES.

from Chicago to Las Vegas at his own expense when he discovered that their schedule would allow a couple of extra days' rehearsal. It paid off, and though this was the last time Sinatra and Basie would record together, the partnership was perpetuated on the concert stage.

THAT'S LIFE

That's Life/ I Will Wait For You/ Somewhere My Love/ Sand And Sea/ What Now, My Love?/ Winchester Cathedral/ Give Her Love/ Tell Her/ The Impossible Dream/ You're Gonna Hear From Me

Sinatra's first attempt to record 'That's Life' with Ernie Freeman, on 25 July 1966, came to nothing, but it was recut on 18 October and the remaining tracks were added a month later. The title song was another huge hit, reaching number 4 in the US though only making the Top Fifty in the UK. In between 'Strangers...' and this he had also charted with Johnny Mercer's 'Summer Wind'. These songs, along with the dreaded 'My Way', whose time was rapidly approaching, the chart-topping 'Somethin' Stupid' hit with daughter Nancy and 1969's 'Love's Been Good To Me', marked an extraordinary singles-chart renaissance in Sinatra's career. The defiant 'That's Life' was in fact a blueprint, in terms of the lyric, for 'My Way' - and to these ears remains a far more acceptable expression of self-satisfaction.

FRANCIS ALBERT SINATRA & ANTONIO CARLOS JOBIM

The Girl From Ipanema/ Dindi/ Change Partners/ Quiet Nights Of Quiet Stars/ Meditation/ If You Never Come To Me/ How Insensitive/ I Concentrate On You/ Baubles, Bangles And Beads/ Once I Loved

1967 began busily, with testimony before a Grand Jury concerning Sinatra's friendship with mobster Sam Giancana and with the two-day session that not only produced this remarkable album but 'Somethin' Stupid' as well. At the core of the album, arranged and conducted by Claus Ogerman, were the compositions of the Brazilian composer Jobim, who also contributed guitar, and vocals on four of the numbers. As befitted the feathery, reedy nature of Jobim's music this was a gentle and romantic set, of which Sinatra observed: "I haven't sung so softly since I had the laryngitis." His voice was perfectly controlled throughout one of the most successful of the Reprise projects.

THE WORLD WE KNEW

The World We Knew/ Somethin' Stupid/ This Is My Love/ Born Free/ Don't Sleep In The Subway/ This Town/ This Is My Song/ You Are There/ Drinking Again/ Some Enchanted Evening

Three of these tracks were recorded in New York on 29 June 1967, half-a-dozen more at a Hollywood session on 24 July, and the addition of the 'Stupid' smash, which topped both the US and UK charts on April 15, made for an attractive but fort-holding package. It was originally released on vinyl under the revealing title *Frank Sinatra*.

FRANCIS A AND EDWARD K

Follow Me/ Sunny/ All I Need Is The Girl/ Indian Summer/ I Like The Sunrise/ Yellow Days/ Poor Butterfly/ Come Back To Me

Maybe this should have been even better, as with Sinatra's two studio collaborations with Basie, but to hear him with Duke Ellington (Edward K) cannot be without pleasure. Billy May was the arranger, and alto-sax master Johnny Hodges provides a number of highlights, notably his solo on 'Indian Summer'. This two-day summit meeting took place in Hollywood during December 1967.

GREATEST HITS VOLUME 1

Strangers In The Night /Summer Wind/ It Was A Very Good Year/ Somewhere In Your Heart/ Forget Domani/ Something Stupid/ That's Life/ Tell Her/ The World We Knew/ When Somebody Loves You/ This Town/ Softly As I Leave You

A 1968 collection from the Reprise years so far that became a top-tenner.

CYCLES

Rain In My Heart/ Both Sides Now/ Little Green Apples/ Pretty Colors/ Cycles/ Wandering/ By The Time I Get To Phoenix/ Moody River/ My Way Of Life/ Gentle On My Mind

This album, with Don Costa as both arranger and producer, was Sinatra's first consistent attempt to come to terms with contemporary writing, and as such was no doubt a great relief to his paymasters at Warner Brothers. The original vinyl issue had a striking cover photograph of a black-suited Sinatra in 'Thinker' pose, and also listed one song ('Wait By the Fire') which didn't make the final cut.

It is, to be honest, a mixed bag, but there are some delights here. Above all, Jimmy Webb's 'By the Time I Get to Phoenix' makes perfect sense as a Sinatra vehicle. Webb had discovered a highly original variation on the 'leaving' theme, and Sinatra probes every nuance with telling understatement. He

also scores with Bobby Russell's disarming little love song 'Little Green Apples', at least forcing a draw with the Roger Miller hit version.

In *Sinatra, His Life and Times* Fred Dellar tells the story of George Harrison visiting the studio and being amazed at the speed at which Sinatra could work. By this time, of course, The Beatles were entrenched in the modern habit of 'creating' in the studio over a period of months, and it must have seemed a long time since they cracked out the début Beatles album in a day!

MY WAY

Watch What Happens/ Hallelujah I Love Her So/ Yesterday All My Tomorrows/ My Way/ For Once In My Life/ If You Go Away/ Mrs Robinson/ Didn't We/ A Day In The Life Of A Fool

The record that unleashed a monster in its title track was recorded in Hollywood in February 1969, with Don Costa as arranger and conductor, Sonny Burke as usual as producer. 'My Way' was a

French song, to which Paul Anka - in probably the most lucrative day's work of his career - contributed an English lyric. It sits in another mixed bag of an album - 'Mrs Robinson' is a particularly insensitive piece of work - but how one reacts to the set as a whole is inevitably coloured by one's opinion of its blockbuster.

Although it only made the 20s in the US charts - no higher than 'Cycles', in fact - 'My Way' has a deliberately anthemic quality that has ever since been associated, perhaps more than any other song, with its creator, as if it represents a defiant slice of autobiography. In the UK it was an instant Top-Tenner for Sinatra, and after its first chart run it kept easing itself back into the list, reappearing for the eighth time on New Year's Day 1972. In total it was in the UK charts for 122 weeks, earning it a longest-ever-run rating from *The Guinness Book of Hit Records*. 'My Way' is either a deep, complex and mature reflection on life, or it's a smug piece of right-wing bombast. This is not my favourite album.

A MAN ALONE

A Man Alone/ Night/ I've Been To Town/ From Promise To Promise/ Single Man/ Beautiful Strangers/ Lonesome Cities/ Love's Been Good To Me/ Empty Is/ Out Beyond The Window/ Some Travelling Music

Sinatra and Don Costa returned to the same studio exactly a month after laying down 'My Way' for a far more cohesive piece of work, one of the great Sinatra albums. The 'concept' could hardly have been a tighter one: not only the writing of one composer, the poet and song-writer Rod McKuen, but a sequence consciously created from the outset by McKuen for this project, as his lyrical statement of where he felt Sinatra was 'at'. At the break-up of his marriage to Mia Farrow, apart from anything else.

Costa was back on form as well, scoring with taste and restraint where the previous album had too often been vulgar. The choice of single was 'Love's Been Good to Me', mature and reflective and an outstanding piece of work, as is 'Empty Is' in particular. Singles buyers in America only eased it as far as 75 in the charts, but in the UK 'Love's Been Good to Me' followed 'My Way' into the Top Ten. Sinatra commented: 'Whatever the man was trying to say in the song[s]... I'd been there and back.' That, of course, is also the impression given by 'My Way', but here Sinatra the great *auteur*, in collaboration with another artist of considerable stature, makes the point with so much more subtlety.

song sequence, about a place in New York state called Watertown, was specifically tailored for Sinatra, and was designed as a TV special about small town life. While not on a par with the McKuen project there are good things here, and yet it was, at least by Sinatra's recent standards, a total failure commercially. Recorded in July 1969, maybe it was simply swamped by continuing attention given to the earlier work, and the chart life of 'Love's Been Good to Me'.

WATERTOWN

Watertown/ Goodbye/ For A While/ Michael And Peter/ I Would Be In Love/ Elizabeth/ What A Funny Girl/ What's Now Is Now/ She Says/ The Train

After the critical and commercial success of A Man Alone, Sinatra turned to another writer and another theme. The writer was Bob Gaudio, a member of The Four Seasons and in partnership with that group's producer Bob Crewe author of most of their hits. Again the

SINATRA IN THE SIXTIES (VIRTUOSO)

The Summit At The Sands (With Dean Martin, Sammy Davis Jr, Joey Bishop And Peter Lawford)/ I Love Vegas/ Talk To Me/ River Stay 'Way From My Door/ Ol' Macdonald/ The House I Live In/ My Blue Heaven/ Without A Song /Imagination/ I'll Be Seeing You/ Too Marvelous For Words/ They Can't Take That Away From Me/ I Have Dreamed/ A Foggy Day/ My Heart Stood Still/ I Get A Kick Out Of You/ Fly Me To The Moon/ You Make Me Feel So Young/ Luck

LEFT TO RIGHT: BOB HOPE, FRANK, BING CROSBY AND JOHN WAYNE.

Be A Lady/ Medley With Sammy Davis Jr/ Goin' Out Of My Head/ It Was A Very Good Year/ Star

A diligent compilation of often-historic rarities taken from the entire decade: the 'Rat Pack' Vegas gig, a Dean Martin TV show, gigs in Sydney, for the UN and in St Louis, a Sammy Davis TV special, an Oakland Coliseum gig and the 1969 Academy Awards ceremony.

SINATRA & COMPANY

One Note Samba/ Don't Go Away/ Wave/ Someone To Light Up My Life/ Desafinado/ Drinking Water/ This Happy Madness/ Triste/ Lady Day/ I Will Drink The Wine/ Bein' Green/ My Sweet Lady/ Sunrise In The Morning/ Leaving On A Jet Plane/ Close To You

Sinatra's last album before announcing his retirement began with a studio reunion with Antonio Carlos Jobim in February, 1969, before the 'My Way' sessions. In November he and Don Costa cut a version of Bob Gaudio's Billie Holiday tribute 'Lady Day', originally designed for the *Watertown* project, and it wasn't until almost a year later, in October 1970, that Sinatra and Costa completed this album, which is half Jobim, half Costa. Apart from 'Lady Day', 'Wave' (arranged as were all the Jobim sides by Eumir Deodato) is perhaps the outstanding achievement of a somewhat ordinary album.

GREATEST HITS VOLUME 2

My Way/ A Man Alone/ Cycles/ Bein' Green/ Love's Been Good To Me/ I'm Not Afraid/ Goin' Out Of My Head/ Something/ What's Now Is Now/ Star/ The September Of My Years

On 23 March 1971 a statement was issued from Sinatra's office: 'Frank Sinatra will retire from show business in June after fulfilling promised engagements.' On 13 June he ended a performance in Los Angeles with the song 'Angel Eyes', the last phrase of which is 'Excuse me while I disappear.' Reprise filled what they naturally hoped (correctly) would be a temporary gap in the supply of Sinatra product with a swift second volume of 'greatest hits'. Some of the tracks hadn't even been singles, and so as is often the case with these compilations, it was more a case of 'somebody at the record company's idea of his best recent numbers'. As such, it's a pretty good selection.

OL' BLUE EYES IS BACK

You Will Be My Music/ Winners Theme/ Nobody Wins/ Send In The Clowns/ Dream Away/ Let Me Try Again/ There Used To Be A Ball Park/ Noah/ You're So Right (For What's Wrong In My Life)

Sinatra's friend Dean Martin happily motored through old age on the golf course, whereas other celebrities whose financial future is secure miss the spotlight - in 1997 the multi-millionaire boxer Sugar Ray Leonard could not resist one more tussle, and Sinatra was clearly not built for the country-club life either. As this night-owl wryly observed: "No fun trying to hit a golf ball at eight at night." His retirement lasted two years.

While still officially retired this former pal of President Kennedy had sung at a Nixon rally, confirming his dramatic political swing from liberal left to the right. It was after singing once again for Nixon, at the White House on 17 April 1973 (see below), that Sinatra said that he had 'retired from retire-ment'. A series of sessions with arranger Gordon Jenkins followed in the summer, and in November his return was marked with a TV special bearing the same name as this comeback album.

On the evidence of this warm and varied selection Sinatra was refreshed and ready to go to work. His wistful reading of Stephen Sondheim's 'Send In The Clowns' made the song his own, though there was enough life in it for Judy Collins to score a hit with it two years later. The voice may have begun to lose the elasticity of youth - after all, he was nearing 60 - but it was proving harder for time to erase his greatest vocal strength, his precise, con-sidered phrasing.

FROM HOBOKEN N. J. TO THE WHITE HOUSE (FREMUS)

Intro (President Nixon)/ You Make Me Feel So Young/ Moonlight In Vermont/ One For My Baby/ I've Got You Under My Skin/ I Have Dreamed/ Fly Me To The Moon/ Try A Little Tenderness/ Ol' Man River/ I've Got The World On A String/ Monologue/ The House I Live In/ Nixon Salute/ You Are The Sunshine Of My Life/ Sweet Caroline/ I Get A Kick Out Of You/ Bad Bad Leroy Brown/ I've Got You Under My Skin/ The Lady Is A Tramp/ Monologue/ Nancy/ My Way

Sinatra's humanitarian, anti-racist and liberal track record is such that it is depressing to remember that he turned out for the sleazebag Nixon, but here is the historic concert. The second half of this CD is a 5 July 1974 performance on board the USS Midway at a naval base in Japan.

FRANK AND DEAN MARTIN AT THE 1959 BASEBALL WORD SERIES IN LOS ANGELES.

SOME NICE THINGS I'VE MISSED

You Turned My World Around/ Sweet Caroline/ Summer Knows/ I'm Gonna Make It All The Way/ Tie A Yellow Ribbon/ Satisfy Me One More Time/ If/ What Are You Doing The Rest Of Your Life?/ Bad Bad Leroy Brown/ You Are The Sunshine Of My Life

Some of the things he had missed were indeed nice, notably David Gates's tender ballad 'If', but Sinatra's song selection faltered for this second post-retirement set, begun in December 1973 and completed in the following spring. Not even he can turn the dreadful chart-topper 'Tie A Yellow Ribbon' into a good song; 'Bad

Bad Leroy Brown' remains the property of Jim Croce; and 'Sweet Caroline' seems to need Neil Diamond's medallion-chested power.

THE MAIN EVENT

The Lady Is A Tramp/ I Get A Kick Out Of You/ Let Me Try Again/ Autumn In New York/ I've Got You Under My Skin/ Bad Bad Leroy Brown/ Angel Eyes/ You Are The Sunshine Of My Life/ The House I Live In/ My Kind Of Town/ My Way

On 2 October 1974 Sinatra began a national tour with the great bandleader Woody Herman and his current band, billed as The Young Thundering Herd, that moved from Boston to Dallas in the course of the month and included a tele-vised date at Madison Square Garden. When this below-par album appeared it claimed to be recorded at the Madison Square gig but it was in fact stitched together from various tour dates, during which the band seemed to be in better shape than the star.

TRILOGY

Past

The Song Is You/ But Not For Me/ I Had The Craziest Dream/ It Had To Be You/ Let's Face The Music And Dance/ Street Of Dreams/ My Shining Hour/ All Of You/ More Than You Know/ They All Laughed

Present

You And Me (We Wanted It All)/ Just The Way You Are/ Something/ Macarthur Park/ New York, New York/ Summer Me, Winter Me/ Song Sung Blue/ For The Good Times/ Love Me Tender/ That's What God Looks Like

Future

What Time Does The Next Miracle Leave?/ World War None/ The Future/ I've Been There/ Song Without Words/ Before The Music Ends (Finale)

Sinatra spent the second half of 1979 working on this ambitious project originally released as a triple album. The concept was straightforward, however: a look back at past repertoire with Billy May, an album of current songs arranged by Don Costa and Nelson Riddle and, the ambitious bit, a new suite by Gordon Jenkins looking to the future. The challenge with the first part, of course, was to breathe new life into familiar material - not all of it, however, from Sinatra's own songbook (this was his first recording of 'My Shining Hour'). The answer was to rely on May's genius for matching Sinatra's easy-swinging, up-tempo mood, and the results are satisfying.

The *Present* album is a more mixed achievement, but the successes are as good as anything Sinatra did in the later phase of his career. In particular, he returns to George Harrison's 'Something', a song for which Sinatra expressed huge admiration and which he first cut in 1970. It is now a masterpiece. Billy Joel's first, huge, hit of two years previously, 'Just the Way You Are', is taken at a canter, a deliberate re-reading of the number. Sinatra recognises country singer/writer Kris Kristofferson's skill at simple, memorable songs of sometimes world-weary experience by choosing 'For The Good Times', treated as an affecting duet with Eileen Farrell. And

Elvis Presley's youthful vibrato ballad 'Love Me Tender' is now gentle and mature.

Anything attempting a task as unusual as does the Gordon Jenkins part of the work is inevitably going to flirt with pretentiousness. To a 'saloon singer' a speculative survey of the future, twisting the mirror around to look back in autobiographical mood, risks disaster. This is averted, though the results are patchy. It is impossible not to be moved, however, as the suite moves towards its climax. Sinatra was now approaching old age, a time when most entertainers have either embraced the country-club life that bored him, or at best are treading water, trading on the past. Sinatra, on the other hand, was still searching, still growing, and that at least must be respected. He reached another landmark on 26 January 1980, between completing the Trilogy sessions and the set's release, when he performed in front of 175,000 people in a Rio de Janeiro stadium - the biggest-ever audience for a solo performer.

SHE SHOT ME DOWN

Good Thing Going/ Hey Look, No Crying/ Thanks For The Memory/ A Long Night/ Bang Bang/ Monday Morning Quarterback/ South To A Warmer Place/ I Loved Her/ The Gal That Got Away/ It Never Entered My Mind

Although on the cover photograph for this 1981 album the Fifties hat has been replaced by a toupee, and the sharp suit by a black leather jacket, the reflective pose, the cigarette smoke and the glass of Scotch suggest that little has changed since those magnificent 'lonely' albums of that distant decade. And there is a consistent theme, now as then: the end of an affair. The connection is explicitly stressed by a return to 'It Never Entered My Mind' from the *Wee Small Hours* album.

But one thing that had indeed changed, it would seem, is his reliable ear for a song. The album title, of course, comes from Cher's big hit of 1966, 'Bang Bang', but what relevance it has to a man in his late sixties remains a mystery. But inevitably there are delights as well: since 'Thanks for the Memory' is really only

known as a throwaway signature tune for non-singer Bob Hope, it comes as a surprise to hear the piece actually sung. It is noticeable that in the Fifties Sinatra went into the studio and emerged two days later with one of his great 'concept' albums, whereas this one was pieced together from sessions beginning on 8 April and ending on September 10. On the other hand, it would be churlish not to note that Sinatra was still trying, still exploring.

L.A. IS MY LADY

L.A. Is My Lady/ The Best Of Everything/ How Do You Keep The Music Playing?/ Teach Me Tonight/ It's All Right/ Mack The Knife/ Until The Real Thing Comes Along/ Stormy Weather/ If I Should Lose You/ A Hundred Years From Today/ After You've Gone

Quincy Jones returned as arranger/conductor for an album cut in both New York and Los Angeles during April and May, 1984, using numerous arrangers and stacking the band with big names like George Benson and Lionel Hampton. But all this talent could not hide the fact that Sinatra's voice was fading fast.

SEE THE SHOW AGAIN
(LABEL UNKNOWN)

Maybe This Time/ See The Show Again/ Searching/ The Pretty Girls I've Never Kissed/ Only One To A Customer/ When Joanna Loved Me/ As Time Goes By/ These Foolish Things/ I'll Never Smile Again/ In The Wee Small Hours/ This Love Of Mine/ But Beautiful/ Let Me Try Again/ Imagination/ All By Myself/ Embraceable You/ I'm Never Gonna Fall In Love Again/ There's Something About You/ Remember/ The Hungry Years/ The More I See You/ Oh Babe What Would You Say?/ Sorry Seems To Be The Hardest Word/ See The Show Again

With tracks drawn from the second half of the 1970s and on up to 1987, this would appear to be out-takes and rejected masters.

SINATRA UNRELEASED
(LABEL UNKNOWN)

Happy Birthday To Me/ Leave It All To Me/ It's Time For You/ My Foolish Heart/ My Foolish Heart (With Frank Sinatra Jr)/ The Saddest Thing Of All/ Body And Soul/ Mack The Knife/ Let's Face The Music And Dance/ Have You Met Miss Jones?/ Cry Me A River (run-through)/ Evergreeen/ Gunga Din

Marked 'Special Limited, Numbered Edition for Private Circulation Only' this CD was released to coincide with Sinatra's 80th birthday and includes TV commercials, and alternate, unfinished and abandoned takes from the entire Reprise period from 'Ring-a-Ding Ding!' to 1988.

THE REPRISE YEARS

In The Still Of The Night/ Granada/ I'm Getting Sentimental Over You/ Without A Song/ I Get A Kick Out Of You/ Night And Day/ Come Rain Or Come Shine/ All Or Nothing At All/ A Nightingale Sang In Berkeley Square/ All Alone/ I Won't Dance/ Ol' Man River/ I've Got You Under My Skin/ In The Wee Small Hours Of The Morning/ Nancy/ The Way You Look Tonight/ Fly Me To The Moon/ All The Way/ Luck Be A Lady/ I Only Miss Her

When I Think Of Her/ September Of My Years/ This Is All I Ask/ It Was A Very Good Year/ Strangers In The Night/ Call Me Irresponsible/ Moon Love/ Don't Worry/ One For My Baby/ My Kind Of Town/ Poor Butterfly/ How Insensitive/ Dindi/ By The Time I Get To Phoenix/ Cycles/ Didn't We?/ Something Stupid/ Love's Been Good To Me/ A Man Alone/ Goin' Out Of My Head/ Something/ Train/ Lady Day/ Drinking Again/ Send In The Clowns/ Let Me Try Again/ What Are You Doing The Rest Of Your Life/ If/ Put Your Dreams Away

Initially released on vinyl in 1986 and later transferred to CD, this was joined in 1990 - as with the similar Capitol collection marking the singer's 75th birthday - by an even more comprehensive four-CD set *The Reprise Collection.*

THE SINATRA SAGA
VOLUME 2 (BRAVURA)

I Sing The Songs/ The Best Is Yet To Come/ Come Rain Or Come Shine/ Change Partners/ I Can't Get Started/ For Once In My Life/ I See Your Face Before Me/ Just The Way You Are/ See The Show Again/ It's All Right With Me/ For The Good Times/ Pennies From Heaven/ Empty Tables/ I'm Never Gonna Fall In Love Again/ The Song Is You/ Angel Eyes/ They All Laughed/ You And Me/ Here's To The Band/ My Way

Out-takes etc: presumably there is a Volume 1 lurking out there somewhere.

LEGENDARY CONCERTS
VOLUME 2
(LABEL UNKNOWN)

Day In, Day Out/ Moonlight In Vermont/ Imagination/ The Moon Was Yellow/ Chicago/ Without A Song/ Willow Weep For Me/ Too Marvelous For Words/ Embraceable You/ I Could Have Danced All Night/ Night And Day/ Ol' Man River/ One For My Baby

Another mysterious 'Volume 2': no details of the actual gigs available.

WITH DAUGHTERS NANCY (LEFT) AND TINA.

Into the Nineties

In 1988 Sinatra joined his old friends Dean Martin and Sammy Davis Jr for what was intended to be a world-tour reunion of the Rat Pack survivors. But after just a few gigs it was obvious that Martin had lost the plot and was beginning to ramble. He was persuaded to quit while Sinatra and Davis continued for a while as a duo. Then Liza Minnelli was booked to replace Martin, and the tour was repackaged as The Ultimate Event. There were a number of dates in 1988 and sporadic revivals of the idea until 1990 when Davis, now stricken with cancer, had, in his turn, to withdraw. Sinatra continued to tour into the new decade, but it was becoming clear that he, too, was feeling the inevitable effects of old age. He would forget lines and miss cues, and in March 1994 he collapsed from exhaustion during a concert. In the following December came the announcement that he was retiring once more - but only from live gigs. This was more than a year after he had released the first Duets album, in itself his first new record in a decade.

DUETS

The Lady Is A Tramp/ What Now My Love/ I've Got A Crush On You/ Summer Wind/ Come Rain Or Come Shine/ New York, New York/ They Can't Take That Away From Me/ You Make Me Feel So Young/ Guess I'll Hang My Tears Out To Dry/ In The Wee Small Hours Of The Morning/ I've Got The World On A String/ Witchcraft/ I've Got You Under My Skin/ All The Way/ One For My Baby

As a recording artist Sinatra had never been too fond of sharing the microphone. Maybe memories of being forced by Mitch Miller to partner Dagmar and a dog impersonator on 'Mama Will Bark', during his deteriorating relationship with Columbia, never left him. And anyway, there seems little artistic purpose in the consummate craftsman of the popular song being double-billed, except for an occasional laugh with old friends or as a family affair with Nancy.

Late in life, perhaps having been told of new technology that meant he wouldn't actually have to share the microphone at all, he changed his mind, and for the first time since 1961 he went into the Capitol studios to cut a record.

On 17 May 1993 the first orchestral tracks were laid down. Splintering the process even further, Sinatra's own contributions (in fact these tracks were to surface on the second *Duets* outing) were intended to be spliced from live performances already in the can. But in July, and again in October, he did go into the studio to provide his vocal tracks for the first album. The choice of material held no surprises, though the positive way of expressing this, as indeed Sinatra did, was that this was a conscious selection of concert-audience favourites taken from a lifetime's work.

The producer responsible for blending everything together was Phil Ramone, and the Ednet system, using digital telephone links, linked the guest vocalists from studios all over the world to Capitol. They were Luther Vandross, Aretha Franklin, Barbra Streisland, Julio Iglesias, Gloria Estefan, Tony Bennett, Natalie Cole, Charles Aznavour, Carly Simon, Liza Minnelli, Anita Baker, Bono and Kenny G.

All this technical jiggery-pokery, bolstering an elderly and perhaps ailing star, was of course a long way from Sinatra in his prime, strolling into the studio, loosening his tie, checking the charts and laying down his magic, totally in command. Now the producer was in charge. And yet it works rather well, and is certainly more than a technical novelty.

DUETS II

For Once In My Life/ Come Fly With Me/ Bewitched/ The Best Is Yet To Come/ Moonlight In Vermont/ Fly Me To The Moon/ Luck Be A Lady/ A Foggy Day/ Where Or When/ Embraceable You/ Mack The Knife/ How Do You Keep The Music Playing?/ My Funny Valentine/ My Kind Of Town/ The House I Live In

As before, this is a mixture of extremely familiar material. Once again it was assembled by Phil Ramone, and this time features Gladys Knight and Stevie Wonder, Luis Miguel, Patti LaBelle, Jon Secada, Linda Ronstadt, Antonio Carlos Jobim, Chrissie Hynde, Willie Nelson, Steve Lawrence and Eydie Gorme, Lena Horne, Jimmy Buffett, Lorrie Morgan, Frank Sinatra Jr and Neil Diamond.

SINATRA 80TH LIVE IN CONCERT

You Are The Sunshine Of My Life/ What Now My Love/ My Heart Stood Still/ What's New/ For Once In My Life/ If/ In The Still Of The Night/ Soliloquy/ Maybe This Time/ Where Or When/ You Will Be Mine/ Strangers In The Night/ Angel Eyes/ New York, New York/ My Way

Pieced together to mark Sinatra's 1995 birthday, with a cover photo of a 1984 concert, this includes a version of 'My Way' with Luciano Pavarotti that was intended for the Duets project. He includes material drawn from every phase of his career.

Conclusion

There are Sinatra enthusiasts to whom nothing less than everything will do: *The Complete Recordings* with Harry James, the Dorsey-Sinatra Sessions 1940-42, the set of Columbia CDs, all 16 Capitol albums and the Reprise trunk. Such a Sinatraphile has no need of this book. At the other extreme, any decent record shop will supply a 'greatest hits' selection to cover each period of Sinatra's career.

This survey, however, is pitched at all levels of enthusiasm in between these two poles. For this final section of the book I have selected a basic Sinatra collection, camped at the equator of enthusiasm.

For most parts of the world, where copyright protection lapses after 50 years, the Charly Digipak *The Kid from Hoboken* is an excellent survey of the early years, to which might be added the 'official' album *16 Most Requested Songs*, covering the Columbia decade.

When we come to the Fifties, the peak of Sinatra's career, I have a problem with compilations (except, of course, for tracks only ever intended as singles), because this was the period when he pioneered the thematic album, the suite of songs exploring a particular mood. Of the 'swinging suicide' pieces

my favourites are *Only The Lonely*, *In The Wee Small Hours* and *Where Are You?*, in that order. As far as the counter-balancing up-tempo sets are concerned, *A Swingin' Affair* was the first fully-achieved, confident album, *Come Fly With Me* showed Sinatra's playful sense of musical humour at its best, and *Songs For Swingin' Lovers* was quite simply a phenomenon.

On Reprise, the first sign that Sinatra could still recapture this density and consistency of mood was the stunning *September Of My Years*, whereas the bravest success was his collection of Rod McKuen songs, *A Man Alone*. *Ol' Blue Eyes Is Back* has, of course, a historic place in this long career, and maybe, just for old times sake, one of the *Duets* albums could be added, whichever you feel has the most attractive guest list.